ep;phany
a literary journal

ep;phany
a literary journal

Editor in Chief	Odette Heideman
Fiction Editor	Tanya Rey
Nonfiction Editor	Cullen Thomas
Poetry Editors	Cassandra Gillig, Ben Roylance
Interviews Editor	Adrienne Brock
Editor at Large	Joel Hinman
Contributing Editors	Martin Edmunds, Karol Nielsen, Martin Rock
Typography & Design	Joe Lops
Copy Editor	Macgregor Card
Managing Editor	Nathaniel Otting
Fiction Readers	Adrienne Brock, Alexander Brokaw, Stratton Coffman, Zachary Fishman, Joel Hinman, Belinda Kein, Ethan Plaue, Daria Schieferstein
Nonfiction Readers	Ed Jenkins, John Szubski, Cullen McVoy, Anna Angelidakis, John Dennehy, Carrie Sheppard
Friends of Epiphany	Bernie and Elsie Aidinoff, Sallie Bingham, Vicky Bjur Literary Agency, Augustus Crocker, The Cook Family Fund, Heleny Cook and Richard Hall, Paul and Marcia Cook, Rebecca J. Cook, Warrren and Brammie Cook, Lavinia Currier, Lisa Dierbeck, Dawn and Andy Eig, Martin Edmunds, Elizabeth England, George Franklin, Irene Goodale, Jeffrey Gustavson, Michele Herman, Edward Hirsch, Remy Kothe, Jefferey Lependorf, Sarah Lutz, John van Rens, Elizabeth Macklin, Heather MacMaster, Roxanna Robinson, Pierre George Roy, Vicki Scher, Richard Smolev, Ken and Michelle Stiller, Jerry and Naomi Neuwirth, Derek Walcott, John Edgar Wideman
Board of Directors	Willard Cook, Lisa Dierbeck, Elizabeth England, Remy Kothe, Lisa Paolella

Epiphany is published bianuually by Epiphany Magazine, Inc. a nonprofit §501(c)(3) corporation.

For submission guidelines please visit our web site at www.epiphanyzine.com

Donations and gifts to Epiphany are tax-deductible to the extent allowed by law.

A one-year subscription is $18; a two year subscription is $34.
To subscribe, please visit our website at www.epiphanyzine.com

The ISBN number is 978-0-9749047-4-0   The ISSN number is 1937-9811
THE WINTER 2013/2014 ISSUE WAS PRINTED BY:
The Sheridan Press 450 Fame Ave | Hanover, PA 17331 www.sheridan.com

MISSION STATEMENT: Epiphany is committed to publishing literary work in which form is as valued as content; we look for writing, wherever it may fall on the spectrum from experimental to traditional, that is thoroughly realized not only in its vision but also in its devotion to artistry. We are especially open to writers whose explorations of new territory may not yet have found validation elsewhere.

All rights reserved. No part of this publication maybe reproduced, transmitted in any form or by any means, electronic, mechanical photocopying, recording, or otherwise without prior written consent of Epiphany Magazine, Inc.

Bookstore distribution is through Ingram periodicals. www.ingramperiodicals.com and
Ubiquity Distributors www.ubiquitymags.com

Epiphany is a proud member of CLMP.

SFI
Certified Sourcing
www.sfiprogram.org
SFI-01075

CONTENTS

[FICTION]

Edith Pearlman 7
    The Descent of Happiness

Benjamin T. Miller 14
    The Crooner

Matthew Socia 41
    Contest

Paul Crenshaw 65
    Blind Date

Douglas Watson 73
    Pink Slip

Ruvanee Pietersz Vilhauer 80
    The Rat Tree

Sara Batkie 106
    Those Who Left and Those Who Stayed

Taylor Fox 139
    Not For Public Display

Miranda McLeod 159
    Trespasser Incident

Elena Ferrante (translated by Ann Goldstein) ... 170
    from The Story of a New Name

[NONFICTION]

Natasha Lvovich 98
    Sandy Chronicles

Casey Wiley 121
    Plantation, Florida

[POETRY]

Simone White 11
 Song Cave
 Was the starchild of Dawoud Bey,
  Glenn Ligon & Mickalene Thomas
 Was a flat breast plate

Kim Vodicka 38
 P o d ❤ n k A n g s t

Kelin Loe 53
 from Toxcin Tocsin! Or The Origins of Kelin Loe!

Andrew Durbin 57
 Warm Leatherette

Shannon Burns 72
 Love of Nude

Laura Goldstein 76
 from Loaded Arc

Debbie Hu 79
 i could bolt could i

Steve Rogggenbook 97
 from I Love Music

Sue Landers 118
 They Will Exist Even When They Won't, Or,
 This Then Will Be A Description Of That Thing

Filip Marinovich 131
 Householder Seehorse

Laura Marie Marciano 137
 after
 sparkle and shine

Cean Gamalinda 154
 recut for b

Jess Dutschmann 167
    Here Is Your Poem About My Insides
    Hoc Accidens

[PORTFOLIO]

Jason Katzenstein 33
    Night Drive

Samuel Tolzmann 52, 75, 96, 105, 133, 134, 136, 169
    Penitent
    Figure under Sheet
    It Came Back
    Drawing Made While Waiting For My Hair To Grow
    Untitled
    Process Piece
    Since Everything Tastes Like Dirt
    Grace

Lydia Conklin 63
    Pom Pom is Loose

Edith Pearlman

THE DESCENT OF HAPPINESS

I was eight—old enough to be taken along on a house call as long as I stayed out of the bedroom or wherever the examination was taking place. I usually eavesdropped behind a door. Little children were sometimes examined on a kitchen table spread with a quilt. In those cases I squatted outside the house beneath a window so I could hear the conversation between doctor and child, all sentence fragments as my teacher would have pointed out. "Hurt here?" "There?" "Started when?" But this Saturday morning my father was visiting an adult, Mr. Workman, patient and friend. Mr. Workman had a bad heart, not as bad as he thought it was, my father had told me, but bad enough to be listened to whenever he phoned.

"Can you catch that syncopation on your receiver?" I could hear Mr. Workman shout.

"No. Sam. Sam! Take the phone away from your chest ..." Silence while Mr. Workman presumably obeyed. "Put it back up to your ear and listen to me. I'm on my way, with my stethoscope."

"Good," said Mr. Workman. "After you listen to my heart with the thing I'll use it to call my Aunt Mary."

So he probably wasn't in too much discomfort.

My father was what you might call a country doctor if by that you meant something sociological: a doctor who practiced both in our small town and in the rural area surrounding it. Or you might mean something more artistic, more Norman Rockwellish—a doctor who drove a car so old that his patients were likely to outlive it, a doctor whose stubby fingers, smelling of cigar overlaid with soap, seemed Velcroed to an old black bag, except this was seventy years ago and Velcro had just been invented and none of us had heard of it. In the trunk of his rattly car he kept a case of medicines, a few of which he always transferred to the house icebox whenever he entered a home, and never forgot to remove on departure. For a while I thought that he never forgot anything at all. But I later figured out that anyone who restricts his own conversation to what he knows—what he knows he knows—will seem to have an extraordinary memory, not to mention a well-stocked mind. My father did know a lot but not everything. He knew mid-century medicine and some botany and not much American history. He knew some chemistry and a lot of anatomy. He didn't know the world of animals or the world of stories—two worlds I considered one, since the only books I read were about horses. He knew my mother. He knew me. He knew Mr. Workman and all his other patients, too.

We drove to Mr. Workman's house in the woods, mostly on dirt roads. The fall had been relentlessly wet, but the rain had stopped the day before. In the moist clearing where my father parked, fallen leaves made the ground slick as oilcloth. An occasional wind shook drops from the branches as if new rain were welcoming us. As we walked down the path from the clearing we could see glimpses of Mr. Workman's elvish house. Its peaked small windows resembled its owner's small eyes and the roof over the door extended widely like his upper lip. A carpenter's bench stood at one side of the front door and a handmade table on the other. You'd think that Mr. Workman was Mr. WoodWorkman, and in fact making furniture was his hobby, but he was a lawyer by profession. He practiced in a one-room office near the court house. He was a bachelor, and lived with a dog I did not like—a large noisy hybrid named John Marshall. John Marshall had a pointed snout and black gums. To me he looked like a wolf—no, he looked like a dog who had reverted to wolfdom and then reverted further back to whatever lupine species preceded wolves. I knew nothing of Darwin then except what my father had revealed to me—that once everything on earth was different from the way it was now, that everything we saw descended somehow from something else—sycamores from ferns, sparrows from flying dinosaurs, Mr. Workman from a chimpanzee—but that last conjecture was mine and I never said it. He had feelings like other animals. I knew from experience that horses could be made glad.

John Marshall too. He barked at all Mr. Workman's visitors, strangers or not. He bounded towards them and stood up on his hind legs and put his paws on the newcomer's chest and then, delicately refraining from licking, gave the visitor a whiff of his dreadful breath. In this way he resembled not the wolves his ancestors had been but the dancer his species might become in a few more centuries of evolution.

"He's saying hello," Mr. Workman often explained to me. "He's extra-friendly but harmless." But he frightened me—I sensed that his harmlessness was only a ploy, like my pretending to play outdoors when I was really listening at the window. Out of sympathy with my fear, Mr. Workman kept John Marshall tethered to a post when I was expected.

But today he had forgotten to tie up John Marshall. Or perhaps John Marshall had learned to undo knots. At any rate, we heard the animal barking as soon as we parked the car, and his barks grew louder as we walked up the path, my father going first with his bag attached to his right hand and his box of medicines under his left arm. I knew that if I kept close to him I'd be safe from John Marshall; but the increasingly louder barks rattled me—this special crescendo told me that while we were nearing him he was nearing us—and in an access of terror I wheeled, turned my back on my father, and ran in the other direction. I would reach the car before John Marshall; I would transform myself into a cat; I would leap onto the rounded roof; I would arch my back and hiss and frighten *him*. But in my hurry to change species I neglected to grow the necessary forelegs. Two-legged, feet slipping, losing a sneaker, I fell onto my human knees and then fell further forward, ending up prone on the wet path. I slipped forward wiggling like an early fish. Then I lay still. John Marshall, having caught up with me, yapped at my feet.

This was the end. I knew there was an end to everything—I had lost grandparents to old age and a schoolmate to accident, and I had seen diseased vegetation, and I had wept more than once over the death of Black Beauty. But this was the end of me. John Marshall would choose a way—would file his teeth back and forth on my nape until he severed my head from my body; or gnaw me to shreds; or simply bite me in an available place and infect me with fatal rabies that he'd caught from a bat.

But I felt calm. If one of these ends was destined for me, if this was the way I was to be punished for eavesdropping and other sins, there was nothing to be done. John Marshall had stopped barking. I could hear him panting at my side. Then he panted into my ear, in three-quarter time I thought—my parents loved to hum waltzes.

Then I stopped considering him. I had landed in such a way that my nose was touching a fallen maple leaf. My eyes followed the leaf's periphery, I traveled its veins, I thought of its grandmother the fern, I remembered that some plants evolved later than earlier plants, well naturally, later was later than earlier, I was no longer making sense, the rabies organisms were already keeping house in my brain.

"Ruthie!" and a pair of strong hands with a soap-tobacco smell picked me up under the arms and lifted me and turned me at the same time, so that my chest was pressed to his, my cheek to his, our two hearts beat as one, maybe in three-quarters time. "Darling, why did you run, you know John Marshall would never hurt you;" and indeed John Marshall was holding my sneaker in his smiling mouth, and Sam Workman, his fingers needlessly gripping John Marshall's collar, was panting a little himself but only slightly; his heart was probably OK this time as it usually was.

I didn't explain—I couldn't, not for years—why I had run. But eventually I realized that I had run because I hoped to be first pursued by John Marshall and then saved by the country doctor who had fathered me, proving that he would always rescue me from danger and forgive my sins while he was doing it. He would protect me as long as he lived, and who knew, he might live forever, and so might I. Death is a physiological inevitability, he had once told me, but I already knew he didn't know everything. Probably Darwin didn't either.

Sam was fine—"the usual tachycardia" said Dad after the examination they let me watch. Then he pocketed his stethoscope and he removed the medicines from the icebox and motioned for me to pick up his bag. We walked down the path to the car. I would never forget that day: the useful fear, the flight, the fall, the distracting leaf, the blessed kindness of John Marshall and Sam Workman and my father. I had never been so happy before. I have never been so happy since.

Simone White

SONG CAVE

I say an imprint of bones
inked-up   at the bottom of the body
someone complains of barrenness
she is spread apart   marks the progress of feminine disease
echolocate why don't you   joints of foot
and ankle which
bend the knee which

creaks   does your pelvis sigh also
to bend
press your black fanning bones into fabric   receive an evidence
entire and open   of hinge,

WAS THE STARCHILD OF DAWOUD BEY, GLENN LIGON & MICKALENE THOMAS

Regarding sweet milk and hellfire
as passable instances of mimesis
it could be said the takedown
was underway   its long tooth descending
immemorially   when you sit
let it not be with roast beast
nor shall Tropicalia disgrace
twenty pounds of lean muscle
Ali never looked better in shades

WAS A FLAT BREAST PLATE

When everyone was moving to Prague
When everyone was moving to Fort Greene
Was colored and that was complete
Reversal of the circumstance of circumference

Encircled   The circle was of being dispersed
Of trying to live
Was Beckett universe a place
Wasn't no one moving there

Was the bresaola to come with from (not Italy)
The colonial last armored location
Was sliding vertically along the hard
Front of economic history

Benjamin T. Miller

THE CROONER

The inventory of summer never changes: cigarettes consuming themselves unattended in a scalloped ashtray, a broken wedge of lime in a gin glass, the hiss of a record that has finished playing still going round. Family means ice cream stains on your merino slacks. The sprinkler chick chick chicks across the yard and the kids run shrieking through it.

Dixon doesn't like these reunions. He prefers situations in which all eventualities have been planned for. Stage lights come up and curtain opens. Snare shot, band strikes in. Applause lights demand fealty from the audience. The set list is final; requests are not considered. Later, a car is waiting. In the car are an approved circle of confederates. The driver doesn't make small talk and sticks to main thoroughfares—no shortcuts.

But this: old faces he vaguely remembers, people from the neighborhood looming up with grins and putting forth sweaty hands, calling him Chuck; he doesn't like it.

It is a ritual that must be observed. Otherwise they will say he has gone Hollywood on them. They'll say the Reds have gotten to him, because everyone knows Hollywood is crawling with Reds, and if not them, the Jews. Who are mostly Reds, anyway. They'll say he has forgotten where he came from: Van Nuys. Nevermind that this is precisely what he has done. There is a code at work here. Family man, no wife, no kids of his own yet (*never let 'em get their hooks in you, Dix,* some wiseguy jokes while his wife wrestles twin boys into the Radio Flyer wagon), but devoted son and brother. Good boy, but not too good. Invite a photographer along. Take a picture of me and ma on the porch. Take one of me and Cliff the window washer. Invite a writer. Write something about how I still buy a cup of coffee at the same place whenever I'm in town.

Everyone has brought with them an expectation. C'mon Charlie, throw a baseball. Set your drink down. Take a dip in the pool—there's an extra suit inside if you want it. He must fend off these entreaties with care. Only when someone's request falls within the natural jurisdiction of celebrity does he relax. He'd love to sign a photograph or a record sleeve. *To Judith, Keep on swinging! Charlie Dixon.* He will be happy to tell that funny story again, the one he told Mack Monday on the Mack Monday Radio Hour last week.

In this way, he can endure.

But a sour note will be struck; it is inevitable. This time it is the arrival of Cate's parents. A pair of lean people in colorless dungarees, his shirt and her blouse each buttoned to the neck despite the warm day. They have come from the garden and their hands are dirty. Dixon experiences a familiar rising anxiety merely at the sight of them entering by the side gate and then stopping at the edge of the yard. They stand apart, satisfying their attendance requirement, content to come no further. Cate's father inspects the leaves of the rhododendron bush for disease, rubbing them proprietarily with his thumb, and then hunkers down to yank a dandelion. Her mother reviews the party with arch disapproval.

Dixon is compelled by decorum to go and greet them. They'd been neighbors all his life on this parched suburban lane. He crosses the thick, green lawn which springs under his feet, navigating children and their toys, stepping over the Rubicon of runoff from their sprinkler. Charles, they call him. Their hands are large and dry, flaked with dirt, offered objectively to shake. Now Dixon's right hand is dirty and he's not sure what to do with it; all afternoon he has been hooking a thumb in the pocket of his slacks and gesturing with the beer bottle in his left hand, a pose from which he can construct a façade of affability.

It seems to Dixon that with their mere presence, Cate's parents have introduced a pervasive uneasiness. Conversation is dampened, laughter is strained. Someone finally notices the hissing of the record and picks the needle up. Just like that, the rules have been overturned, all of his careful arrangements nullified. Cate's parents have always been difficult, a pair of Okies, a rebuke to the community; studied churchgoers, heavily mortgaged on a modest house with a scrupulous garden, carrying themselves with a stiff and condescending pride in their plain clothes and battered automobile. Cate has not spoken to them in nearly three years, and something she once said of them resonates in Dixon's mind: "They think that being worse off than everyone else makes them better."

But there has been a further complication since Dixon last saw them. Word came from Korea that their son, Cate's brother, was lost, quite literally—his whereabouts are unknown. It has been two weeks, and there has been a voluminous lack of confirmation. He is neither alive nor dead. The army simply fails to find him. This bestows on them a type of dire neighborhood celebrity with which Dixon cannot compete. Dixon's own brother is serving in Korea, officially, though strings have been pulled and presently he is carrying gasoline canisters on a base in Germany. So the attention of the party is upon their little triumvirate, and Dixon is afraid to inquire about the latest news, and afraid not to. He compromises by asking how they've been keeping, an innocent query that nonetheless suggests tragedy, and he is momentarily proud of this strategic approach.

"Oh, getting along," is their uniform reply.

Dixon is relieved. He can say, "Good, glad to hear it," and imply that he comprehends their submerged sorrow without having to actually say it. One or two more such shrewd pleasantries and he may be able to disengage.

Then Cate's father says, "Imagine you heard about Kenneth," while simultaneously reaching out and pinching the fabric of Dixon's sleeve with thumb and forefinger, rubbing it disdainfully as though it were a sickly rhododendron leaf. "That's a fine shirt."

Dixon suddenly feels ridiculous, like a puffed-up sissy in his merino slacks and polished shoes and tailored tee-shirt. These people, this assembled party, have known him all his life, have seen him scared on the first day of school and pushing a mower in the front lawn. They have seen him scratching his pimples. They see through him, Dixon is certain. He's just a dandified hick from the Valley playing at being a star. While other men are doing honest work. While real men are in Korea with rifles in their hands.

It does not help that he is painfully in love with Cate. It preys on his every waking hour. And now with her estranged parents here before him (it is Cate who enforces the embargo, who cannot bear their eyes upon her), the effect is magnified. Dixon is only vaguely aware of the party continuing softly behind him, of low conversation, the rasp of a match, someone opening a bottle and the bottlecap clicking on the flagstone. He finds himself sweating. Nothing makes Charlie Dixon sweat.

"Yes," he says finally. "I heard about Kenneth. Is there any news?"

Cate's father makes an indistinct sound, perhaps it is a thin laugh, and smiles mirthlessly. "No news."

"Oh. Well, I—"

"You what?"

"I—I don't know."

"That's all right, Charles. Looks like you've got a party to tend to. Don't let us keep you."

There is a spectral hand around his throat. He will never sing again.

Dixon doesn't like these reunions.

Evening falls and he has done his duty. His leased Buick is in the driveway, blockaded by other vehicles. There are child-sized handprints on the glossy hood and smudges where they have pressed their noses against the glass. He wipes it with a clean rag while he waits for men to shamble around from the backyard and move their cars.

"Don't worry, Chuck," they call subserviently, "we'll have 'em out of your way in no time."

He smiles. "Thanks a million, fellas."

The farewell is another ritual that must be handled with delicacy. Immediate family musters on the porch: mother and father, two sisters, their husbands, their children. Only Dixon's brother is absent. Writer and photographer hover nearby. Dixon must spend enough time on each of them. Begin with the smallest, an infant, and move up through the ranks to the eight-year-old sandy-headed nephew (*Keeping on swinging, champ!*). Then his sisters. Both of them had their hair done for the occasion, by this time undone by the harassments of sun and wind. He shakes hands with their husbands. Frank, Bob, always a pleasure. Then his parents.

"Don't stay away so long next time," his mother says. "It's only Van Nuys, not the dark side of the moon."

"Jeez, ma." He rolls his eyes for the photographer and the writer. "You'd think I just lay around all day with nothing to do. Anyway. Take care, pop."

The photographer's camera clicks without rest.

Then he is driving back into the city, and thinking about Cate. Driving is another pastime he does not enjoy. His attention wanders and he is forever braking sharply to avoid accidents. It is a strange night. Foggy, even this far from the ocean. Coming through the hills into Hollywood he can hardly make out the scaffold lights on the new tower they're building for Capitol Records on Vine Street, a great tubular thing inside of which he can see himself eventually feeling quite at home. There will be lush carpets and stiff leather sofas. You will need to be a certain kind of person to access the expansive upper floors, though tonight they are just skeletal girders and rebar. He is beginning to recover from the afternoon. Thinking about signing with Capitol makes him feel better. He imagines how heavy the pen will be. The unfinished building soars closer and the fog consumes it all but for the brave yellow lights.

Cate lives in Santa Monica—so, this will be her pretext. They're socked in. Not safe to leave the house, nothing to do but send a note to Mr. and Mrs. Dixon with her apologies. She always got along with his parents, seemed to enjoy their mild geniality, which, he supposes, is why she still goes to the effort of inventing an excuse whenever one of these soirees passes her by. He'll call her when he gets home. It's good this way. Puts him in command of their next encounter. He can report on the Van Nuys crowd: Nothing changes. Yeah, sure, your folks were there. Sure, I talked to them. Oh, you know, same old story. Listen, forget them; let's you and me have dinner in the city.

His house in the Hollywood hills is cleverly concealed by foliage and by a pair of aristocratic iron gates. But the house itself is not as large or splendid as these flourishes are designed to suggest. In fact, it is pretty ordinary, and not even his. He is renting, and this fact consoles him. A mansion with its endless echoing passageways doesn't interest him. Money and property invariably fail to hold his attention. It is only the impression of fine things that entices him; the impression they make on others. (He remembers with a twinge, quickly suppressed, Cate's father's beige work shirt buttoned up to his red, weathered neck.)

The house he inhabits is plenty spacious and comfortable for a single man with a traveling lifestyle—that was just how the agent put it. This assessment pleased him. Renting is the smart play for a man in his position. And it gives him a feeling of transience that he enjoys. The house is a waypoint on a long road whose waypoints grow increasingly grand.

First things first: put the Buick away in the garage. Next, change out of these clothes. Sit and have a drink. Consider the opulent strata of light passing through bourbon. Then, a call from his manager: bad news. "Keep on Swinging" has faded from the charts in France and England. But there's a silver lining. Potential in the Latin market.

"They want you to record it in Spanish," he says. "Don't worry, we'll get it written out. All you have to do is sing what's on the page."

"Make sure they have it clean," Dixon says. "No mistakes. I don't want to sound like a fool."

"It'll be clean. How was the family thing?"

"Fine."

"Did the reporter show?"

"He showed."

"Okay, Dix. As long as he showed. You can never tell with these reporters. Listen, I'll be in touch."

There is no answer at Cate's number. A mix of relief and fury. She's gone out in the fog. Gone to the movies, something with Alan Ladd or one of those types. He can imagine her there in the dark, the only soul in the movie house on a night like this—they were going to cancel the show but she is on friendly terms with the manager and he has gone up to the projection room and put it on the reel himself. He can imagine her there, hiding. Alan Ladd squats on a bluff and grabs a handful of soil and lets it crumble through his fingers while his eyes scout the horizon. Cate is beside herself. She loves the safe harbor of the celluloid picture, its unimpeachability, its perfect orchestration. She loves forfeiting herself to it. Every film is perfect in her mind. And as long as her attention remains total, she is perfect. She cannot be breached or broken. She is immune, invincible, and this feeling will not wane until the screen goes black and the studio's pompous coat of arms appears, so bright that when you close your eyes it remains seared in your vision.

The phone rings on into eternity. Cate is off somewhere being perfect in the fog. The morning—he'll call again in the morning, and she'll answer.

The car arrives at nine o'clock to take him to the club. Cocoanut Grove at the Ambassador on Wilshire Boulevard. Not headlining tonight—he's between hits. It is important to stay on stage however he can. Sinatra's in Miami Beach so he can get away with singing a few Sinatra tunes.

The stage manager meets him at the side entrance and a bouncer holds the door open, admitting him into the club's smoky corridors.

"Who's here tonight?"

"Hot crowd, Dix."

"Who's here?"

"A lotta young stars. People on the way up."

"Any names?"

The stage manager clutches his derby hat. "It's Sunday—you know. And with this weather. Jimmy Stewart's people called. He's still on the lot, but might come by."

Yes, he might come by, Dixon thinks. But not likely. And certainly not in time for my set.

Rye whiskey and two cigarettes. Tuxedo is donned, shoulders brushed. Hair pomaded. House lights down, stage lights up. Snare shot, band strikes in. A whoop from the crowd as they recognize the tune. Another whoop as Dixon strides from the wings to the microphone. Wave to the right, wave to the left. Smooth the front of the jacket with a palm. Mouth the words *thank you*. Sing.

Keep on swinging, babe, just swing away
Keep on swinging and you'll get my love someday

He feels good. Right away his voice is true; after the day he's had it might have been ragged at first. The club is full, though he doesn't see many familiar faces. Perhaps that's all right. His manager insists that it's the starlets who are the real tastemakers. If they like your song, everyone trying to get in bed with them will buy a copy. At any rate, he's been coasting on "Keep on Swinging" for too long. "Lucky Old Moon" and "Ain't That Love?" failed to make an impression. The Spanish version could be nice money, but what's he going to do—play some greaser club in East L.A.? Maybe he could sing it for the king and queen of Bolivia or one of those countries.

Four songs in and the crowd is with him. One more up-tempo

number and then time for a ballad. Spot on him. The band backlit in red. He'll do "Smoke Gets in Your Eyes," and Sinatra will never be the wiser. He doesn't scoop the pitch like Sinatra, either. He can really hit the notes. You don't say that to Frank's face—as a matter of fact, you don't say it aloud to anyone. Not if you want to stay in the business. But Dixon can really hit the notes.

Something has happened, though. He can feel their interest recede, a palpable change in the barometrics of the room. Something passes through the dance floor like a temblor. Then a gleaming dome of hair, a tall, gliding figure in a pinstripe suit shown to a table. Well, thinks Dixon, I'll be damned. Stewart has come after all. He gives the waiter a drink order and then nods to Dixon as if giving him permission to continue. Of course, the song has not faltered. But it's as though they all went silent; Dixon has the impression that if they played back the recording there would be fifteen seconds of dead air. He finishes the tune and everyone looks to Stewart for a cue.

He claps politely.

They all clap politely.

Dixon sweeps an arm over the band and asks for a round of applause—sometimes this reels them back in. But no dice. They clap politely.

He sings "Smoke Gets in Your Eyes" and "Mack the Knife" and "Ain't Misbehavin'." Then he takes a bow, waves to the gallery, blows a kiss, takes another bow. Stewart claps his hands twice and begins talking to someone. House lights up, stage lights down. As soon as the curtain is closed the band disassembles itself.

He changes out of the tuxedo, and the circle of approved confederates is waiting for him in the car, with their predictable nicknames: Shep, Duck, Burnsy, and so forth. It is not that Dixon likes these men. But in their vanity, stupidity, and obeisance they are comforting. Their suits and sideburns are correct. Their grasp of protocol is keen. Shep, or perhaps Duck, is handy with names and faces. Dixon doesn't have to worry about them; they never draw on the reservoir of his attention. He doesn't know where they go or what they do when they are not with him. Their patter is as familiar to him as one of his own songs. He could recite it from memory.

"Hot set, Dix." "Yeah, Dix. Great set." "How about Stewart walking in like that?" "Just walking right in, and on a Sunday. To see Dix." "Why the hell wouldn't Jimmy Stewart come in on a Sunday night to see Dix?" "No reason. I'm just saying, on a Sunday." "It was a great set, didn't I tell you it was a great set? Jimmy Stewart's *lucky* to catch a set like that."

They could continue this way seemingly forever, but Dixon speaks, puncturing the flow. Typically he doesn't insert himself until someone asks a direct question. "Where's Burnsy?" he asks. The quorum is incomplete. He feels most comfortable when all are accounted for.

"Oh, Burnsy? He's not here? Hell, I don't know. I can find out. Give me a minute and I'll find out."

"I coulda sworn Burnsy was here. Maybe he found himself a girl," someone says. "We'll ask around, Dix."

"Just give us a minute, Dix, and we'll round him up."

Dixon waves to indicate that no one should expend any effort on the search. The others are happy enough to forget the whole thing.

"What do you think, then, Dix? Where to?"

This is his natural point of entry. The captain has been looked to for an order, and the rank and file are anxious for motion. But Dixon is irresolute. Perhaps he is tired, though it's not a feeling he used to. He does not seem to require much rest, can stay up late and rise early without difficulty. When he sleeps it is largely from a sense of obligation. No, he's not tired, he simply would rather be alone.

"Listen, fellas," he says, "you'd better get out. I'm going home."

The mood in the car deflates. Without him, their prospects for the evening are sharply dimmed. They are a portrait of displeasure prudently concealed.

"Sure thing, Dix. Whatever you say. No problem. Find us if you change your mind."

In the morning, just as he predicted, Cate answers her telephone.

"We missed you at Cocoanut Grove last night."

"Save it. I'm not any of your scum, Charlie Dixon." Her tone is bright, nearly ecstatic. He has caught her when she's up. This is dangerous; she's in an overpromising mood. "As if wild horses could drag me into that gaudy place."

"How about dinner?" he says. "Make it up to me."

"Of course I'll have dinner with you, Charlie. I'll have dinner with you anytime. But I don't have to make up for anything. You know perfectly well—"

"Yes, I know perfectly well. You're not any of my scum."

"Don't act hurt. I didn't mean anything by that."

"I know perfectly well," Dixon says.

He picks her up at seven o'clock in the Buick. It's a shabby little place she's got, really. Riddled with holes, crumbled by salt. He wants to ask her what the hell she lives all the way out here for, but there's no point. She'll only say, in that bright tone, inviting him to disagree, that it's none of his business where she lives. She'll only say: What should I do, Charlie, come and live in Hollywood with you?

Dixon did ask her to marry him once. They had been eighteen, straight out of high school; in fact, still wearing their graduation gowns.

After the ceremony they had gotten into his father's car, honking, waving, etc., and driven to Santa Monica for a party—the same drive Dixon is now undertaking in his Buick. While their friends, some of whom were Eagle Scouts, built a bonfire, they walked on the beach with their gowns on. He had wanted very badly to undo the two chintzy strings at her throat and see what was underneath, although he knew that it was the purple chiffon dress that stopped just above her funny little knees, what she called her good dress. But he wanted to see the graduation gown fall in the sand. He wanted to take the mortarboard hat from her head and sail it into the ocean. He wished to be the kind of guy who did things like that. You fling a woman's hat into the ocean; what can she do about it? She can only be astonished. But he was not that kind of guy. For him women projected a zone of inviolate sanctity—he never could master the custodial gestures that his fellow crooners were so good at, the hand landing on the small of the back or taking hold of the elbow, the intricate messaging of the eyebrows.

So he clasped his hands behind his back and spoke. He hadn't known he was going to do it until he had begun. His voice was already a very good voice. It had survived puberty and made a graceful transit from alto to soprano. He had won every town prize since the eighth grade. His voice was an instrument of power and pliability. There was nothing it couldn't do.

He said: "I love you, Cate."

"Charlie Dixon, behave yourself."

"I'm crazy about you. Let's get married. I want to marry you."

"Charlie," she complained, leaning against him jockishly, "quit kidding around."

"Who says I'm kidding? I'll take you to Hollywood with me."

"You look like a professor in that gown. Come on, Charlie, that's serious stuff. You shouldn't joke about it. Oh, the sun's going down."

She scampered down to the waterline, toward the sunset and away from him.

Dixon perceived the reality of the situation instantly. She would not accept; better to let her think he had been joking. As a matter of fact, hadn't it been sort of a joke? Here they were graduated and hungry for the world and he's talking about marriage? He watched the sunset with her to buy a moment for the lance of misery to pass through, and then he said: "You're right. I can't help it if I'm a kidder. It's getting dark; we ought to turn around soon."

Seven years have elapsed, and Dixon has had his share of women, including a few who dropped slavish hints about how pleased they would be to look down at their finger and see a diamond. But his love for Cate has persisted, divorced from reason. No one has come along to topple the dread throne she sits on. He can lie awake nights on end trying to talk himself out of it. She is too tall and bony in the hips. Tends to cut her hair boy-short. She is indifferent toward music and thoughtless with people; all her sensitivity is reserved for tall, dark heroes who spend most of their time in silhouette.

But none of this seems to matter. When he is with her he feels calm. He can think of her at nine years old with her bobby socks held up by a dab of soap, and at fourteen with her hair losing its blonde and tied with ribbons in two pigtails, and at twenty-one smoking an entire pack of clove cigarettes in a movie theater watching Monty Clift in *A Place in the Sun*. The hanging file of his memory has these images readily available, and they spring at him without warning. Her presence is the only salve for his worries. When they are together, just the two of them, when he has had time to formulate a plan and usher her into it, he experiences serenity. Looking at her, listening to her babble, soothes him. It is like the transport of being onstage, of singing into a supple crowd with the obedient backing of a band.

They don't see each other regularly; lunch, coffee, a movie, sporadic outings carefully arranged. However, she finds ways to compound his misery, always phoning up to inform him of her latest beau. She seems to regard this almost as a public service, and why shouldn't she? He's her friend; he ought to know. Before she's even said anything, there's a certain besotted note in her voice that he has learned to recognize. A jet of pain travels through him, from intestines to frontal lobe. Dixon has become practiced at the art of masking his agony while giving her no encouragement. He grunts, says things like 'uh huh.' Not that she needs any encouragement; Cate will give him the fellow's particulars either way. The man in question is always six-foot-two and clean cut, but not too clean, not like some stuffy lawyer, though he is a lawyer, and he spends the summer surfing at Trestles, but he's not one of those beach bums. At first she thought he was a bit of a dud, but he's really a pretty nice guy if you get to know him. He has a wonderful pet dog. Dixon wishes her good luck and finds a reason to get off the line.

None of her boyfriends have lasted, to his relief. Before long she is seeing movies alone again, hailing the manager to get off his stool and fire up the projector for her, even after the night's last show is over.

She is in one of these unattached lulls now. And Dixon has decided, driving west on Wilshire Boulevard, that he will make a pass. It's what he should have done on graduation day. If he had been more sensible, he probably could have untied those chintzy strings and dropped her gown and found a secluded place to take off the chiffon dress and lay her down in the sand still warm with the sun. That's what anybody else would have done; that would have been the smart play. Think how everything would be different. She'd never be able to hit him in the shoulder and say *Oh, Charlie* after that. She'd never be able to say she was none of his scum.

He arrives at the shabby little apartment and she is not ready, clattering around in high heels searching for her pocketbook and her good earrings. Dixon makes himself a drink; this could take a while. All the time she is shouting from the bedroom about the movie she saw last night. Not Alan Ladd after all, but Henry Fonda. Same pale blue eyes. It was a war picture, but not one of those serious war pictures, one of the funny ones, and she had loved it unconditionally. Fonda played a pilot, or a submarine captain. You should've seen him—you've should've seen the part where—

Dixon's focus wanders until it is time to go. She finally presents herself: shimmery black dress and a white satin band on her head. Luckily there's a bow in it, or else it would look like she'd broken her skull.

"Nice duds, Charlie." She pinches his new gray worsted wool jacket, between thumb and forefinger. A dry kiss on his cheek, smelling of perfume and sweet tobacco. "Shall we?"

On the way back into the city she finishes her account of the Fonda movie, and then says, casually, "Oh, did you hear? They found Kenneth."

Dixon has been focusing on driving and on his plan, so at first he doesn't register this. There is no fog tonight, only a lot of traffic heading into the city, which rises glittering out of the dusk.

"Huh?"

"I said, they found Kenneth. He wasn't dead or anything. Only in the wrong place, the silly boy. Somebody mixed up his paperwork."

Dixon knows he ought to acknowledge the gravity of this news, but can only say: "When?"

"Just this morning. Well, it was last night over there, or tomorrow perhaps—I can never keep it straight."

"That's terrific. You must be so relieved."

"Oh. Yes, I am. I am. Well, not really. I knew they'd find him. Silly boys like Kenneth never die."

He is glad to reach the valet stand on Hollywood Boulevard, to cede the car into their hands. Night has come down just on cue. The sidewalks are full. Searchlights grope the sky. The bulbs on theater marquees make patterned waltzes. Cate grasps his arm and asks where they're going, though she already knows. The calculus is simple. The Formosa Café is a small joint, and it's Sinatra's turf; even though Frank is in Miami Beach, playing the Fontainebleau, sporting cream golf shorts and wading with dignitaries in the warm sea, it's still his turf. He has watchful lieutenants. There's only one other place to be seen.

Musso & Frank Grill: a respectable turnout. Studio heads are in the rear. Screenplay hacks prop up the bar. Chaplin is at his reserved table, bent over liver and beans. No telling who some of these other people might be. They have an important air—and they dress like bums so they must not have to impress anybody.

As he holds open the door, Dixon suddenly stops her and says, "Cate—" but is unable to finish his thought, which was something to do with Kenneth. "If there's anything—you know, my brother is over there."

"Don't tell me they lost him, too."

"No, no, I don't think so—"

"I'm only teasing, Charlie. Are you going to let me inside or what?"

Their table is decent. Not great, but decent. Far enough from the screenplay hacks to avoid being infected by their particular brand of melancholy, the sweat of overdue rent and the sad smudges of typewriter ink on their thumbs. Close enough to the studio heads that one of them could look over and rub the whiskey fog from his eyes and say, "There's that Dixon kid. That Dixon kid's not bad looking and he can really hit the notes. Somebody ought to put him in a picture." And they are in proximity to the bums, the elbows worn glossy on their coats, ugly ties hanging askew. Just no way to know who the bums might be. Not singers or actors, that's for sure. Not songwriters, either. They have their own ghettoized saloon someplace on Yucca, where the jukebox has been broken since 1912 and nobody can stand to hear another song in their lives anyhow. The bums: whoever they are, they must carry some weight to show up at Musso & Frank dressed like that.

Dixon orders for both of them. This is the first stage of his plan, to demonstrate that he knows what she likes to drink and what she likes to eat. And that if she's in the mood for something different, he doesn't especially care. This is no democracy. It is his agenda they're following. So she'll have a vodka martini, up, and a dinner salad. Ribeye for him, and bourbon on the rocks.

"You'll never guess who—"

Then Cate does something that catches him off guard. She interrupts him and says: "Thank you for this, Charlie. It's nice of you."

"What is?"

"Taking me out like this. Showing me a good time. It's nice. I *do* miss you terribly."

"Ah. Well, that's fine." He is nearly derailed by a rush of pleasure. "That's fine."

"You were saying?"

The waiter, in his red jacket that at Musso & Frank always seems to be ill-fitting, along with the faded wallpaper and the darkly lacquered wood part of the mystique of the place, brings their drinks.

"Does it bother you," Dixon asks, "all these old gents walking around with jackets that don't fit?"

"I'd never noticed," Cate says.

He puts a cigarette between her lips and lights it. Then one for himself. Cate is not the noticing kind, unless the thing to be noticed exists within a frame of celluloid. Then she is a true eagle-eye. Nothing escapes her gaze. He has been to the movies with her many times over the years and it amazes him that the same squirm of excitement still overcomes her when the tread of the prison guard can be heard and the hero is scrabbling at the tunnel beneath the wall, when his fingers break through to daylight, when the whistles begin to blow. Afterwards she'll say, did you see the pin on his collar?—it was the same one his father gave him all those years ago. And Dixon will have to admit that he didn't catch it.

"I was saying," he resumes, "you'll never guess who swung by the club for my set last night."

"Who's that?"

"Jimmy Stewart."

"Did he? How nice."

Dixon is perplexed. He thought that would make more of an impression. "Yeah," he says, "it was him. Came straight from the lot."

"He must've been tired, the poor man. Isn't it disappointing—when you see them, I mean—isn't it disappointing how ordinary they are? How they get tired and start to sag just like the rest of us."

"Ordinary? Stewart's as big as they get."

Cate yawns. "I'm sorry I missed your party yesterday, Charlie."

"I never expected you to be there. Besides, it wasn't my party."

"Every party is your party."

"What's that supposed to mean?"

"Oh, you just can't expect me to have too much fun sitting with my feet in the pool while everyone fawns over the great Charlie Dixon."

"I told you, I never expected you to be there. And it's not like that."

"I know what it's like. Don't worry, darling. I'm proud of you. Just like everybody. We're all tremendously proud."

This is not going the way he would like. He thought they would talk about harmless things for a while, get a couple of drinks in, then his hand could wander towards hers, take up her pinky. It's something he saw an A&R man do once, a real slick customer: take up a woman's pinky in such a way that he could caress it, and break it if he wanted to.

Instead, she is proud of him. Her tone is the one you'd use with a child who has aced his spelling test. She adjusts the bow on that ridiculous headwrap, and says:

"I'll make the next reunion, I promise."

"The hell you will." He means this remark to come off as the kind of wry, world-weary thing Jimmy Stewart would say. But instead it sounds like he means it, which he does.

She laughs ringingly. "Oh, you're right. I won't."

"I know. You aren't any of my scum."

"They *are* scum, Charlie, and you know it."

"Who is?"

"The whole Van Nuys crowd. I'm too good for them, and so are you."

"I'm not too good for anybody. I don't forget where I came from," Dixon says.

"Save your breath, Charlie. The *LIFE Magazine* people aren't here now. It's just me."

There is something thrillingly aggravating and sexy about hearing her talk this way. She's right, of course; he has spent many hours perfecting a facsimile of devotion to his hometown, those five eternal miles north, to gathering props, a dime for the right cup of coffee and a dry cleaning ticket for the old letterman jacket. But those humps wouldn't know the Ambassador Hotel if it fell over on them. They'd go to pieces if they ever saw the inside of Cocoanut Grove on a Saturday night. If they caught a glimpse of Cary Grant in a broad-breasted suit doling out hundreds from a thick bend of bills and saying, "Hell of a show, Dix. You were cooking tonight." And the girls with soft dark faces and long legs to break your heart. If they knew what some of those girls were capable of.

He is an initiate into this world. He has crossed over. And to go back to Van Nuys and the sprinklers chick chick chicking and the pink scalloped ashtrays from the Sears & Roebuck catalogue is like being cast out of Olympus. No one down below knows how to behave. The gods are vain and cruel but they live by certain precepts. They don't come up to you sticking out a dirty hand. Once you've grown accustomed to their presence, their ruthless divinity, you cannot bear to leave it.

"Listen" he says, "here's an idea. Why don't you come back to my place after dinner? There's a couple of new records—we just cut 'em the other week. I'll play the masters for you."

"Of course, I'd love to hear them. You'll be a perfect gentleman, I'm sure."

"The trick to being a gentleman is knowing when to stop being a gentleman."

"What fine distinctions you draw, Charlie Dixon."

"As a matter of fact, you ought to move into the city—"

"Don't start with that again."

"I don't mean you should live in an SRO downtown with a bunch of dope fiends. But there's no reason for you to be way out there by the ocean. How's a guy supposed to see you?"

"And you want to see me?" Cate is doing coquettish things with the corners of her eyes.

"Always."

"Well, you'd never know it. If I didn't phone you up we'd be perfect strangers by now."

"Move into the city."

"I'll think about it."

"Don't think about it. Thinking'll just get you into trouble."

"Why do I feel like *you're* going to get me into trouble?"

"I never got anybody into trouble."

"Don't think you can charm me, Charlie Dixon. I'm wise to you. And I like my life the way it is."

"You and I both know that isn't true."

She straightens imperiously. "Why shouldn't I like my life just as it is?"

"All I meant was, if you were in the city—"

"What's so great about the city, anyway? All these cars bumper to bumper, and you can't sleep for the noise."

"You want to be a secretary and go to the movies alone until you die?"

"Is there something wrong with being a secretary?"

"No, there's nothing wrong with it, for a certain sort of person—"

"It's better than being Frank Sinatra's lickspittle."

Dixon is stunned. "Lickspittle?"

"That's what I said, Charlie."

"I'm nobody's—" he begins, and then words fail him. He looks at the cigarette in the ashtray, the bourbon which has left a system of wet rings on the tablecloth, the polished cutlery, and feels the growth of a thick, winding hatred with no clear object.

"Not to be rude," Cate says. "But what you said about—"

"I'm nobody's lickspittle. Nobody's. Do you hear me?"

"Listen, I shouldn't have said that. I was just cross for a minute. What you said about being a secretary—"

"Least of all Frank," Dixon continues, practically shouting now. "Don't talk to me about Frank Sinatra. I'm not his lickspittle or anybody else's. Everything I have, I worked for it. Don't talk to me about Frank Sinatra. He can't hit the notes like I can. Listen to him scoop the pitch. If it wasn't for his dago friends—"

"Charlie, keep your voice down."

"He can't hit the notes so he scoops them, and they say he's got a million dollars. And you. You think you're better than me? You think you could get a table here," he gestures broadly, "any fucking night of the week without me?"

Cate is looking at him, eyes wide. They are all looking at him. The screenplay hacks at the bar, shot glasses suspended an inch from their mouths. Studio heads, who are thinking it's been a while since somebody had a good old-fashioned collapse over dinner. Chaplin stays bent over, but everyone knows he doesn't miss a trick. And the bums. The bums take a good long look. The bums are drinking top shelf booze and eating filet mignon rare, so they aren't bums. Dixon glares at each of them in turn, and they glare back. They have no fear of him. He doesn't rate in their world, whatever world that is. Except that now he's gone and said some things about somebody who does rate.

One by one, they turn away and life resumes. His transgressions have been noted in the official record. The chime of cutlery and rumble of conversation rises.

"I wonder just who the fuck you think you are," he says, speaking almost to himself now. "I take you out for a nice dinner, and this is what you do. You insult me to my face. Call me a lickspittle."

"Charlie—"

"I do my best every damn day since the age of five. Nothing's ever good enough. I try and try."

Dixon's hands are shaking. He tries to retrieve his cigarette but instead he fumbles it into the grime of the tray.

"All I do is love you. Day and night, year after year. All I've ever done is love you the best I can. What do you do? Turn up your nose and insult me to my face."

A waiter, deaf and blind to their strife, materializes with dinner—they do that here, approach with stealth, some trick of their baggy red jackets. Her bountiful salad, food enough for three Cates, and his islet of steak in its bleeding sea.

"Charlie," Cate says eventually. "I didn't know you felt that way."

"Didn't know I felt what way," he mutters darkly, sawing into his steak for something to do, though his appetite is gone and the food turns his stomach.

"That you felt that way—about me."

"You fucking ought to know it."

She says nothing.

"I asked you to marry me, didn't I?"

"But—but that was so long ago. And you were just—you were only fooling—"

He sees understanding come into her face. It feels like a stiletto blade searching his insides.

"Oh, Charlie."

"Forget it."

"I'm so sorry."

"Don't be sorry."

"Charlie, I mean it. I am so—"

Dixon snaps his knife and fork down. He sits for a long moment and then pounds the table, making everything jump.

"Be anything but sorry. I don't need your sorry."

"Oh, Charlie," she says.

"Be quiet and eat."

The drive back to Santa Monica is fast and funereal. The Buick roars with health. Yellow streetlights whip by at dependable intervals, and Dixon finds himself nearly mesmerized by them. The ocean looms up, seeming almost vertical and flat, like the unassailable walls of some further city.

Idling in the car outside of her door, Cate says cautiously, "You can come in for a drink, if you like."

Dixon laughs and pulls the knot of his tie loose. "So that's how it'll be."

"Charlie, I just thought you'd like a drink."

"That's how it is, then. Take pity and throw a little my way."

"No, please, don't say that. I hate for it to be like this."

"How should it be?"

"I don't know. You've given me a terrible shock tonight. I can't—I just need some time to think."

"Take all the time you want."

"Don't be angry with me."

"Can I still have that drink?"

"If you want it."

Dixon smiles. "You're really nothing but a low-rent slut, aren't you?"

Her breath catches. No one has spoken like that to Cate before—not even her parents, who have said such things only in their private way, with the boundless superiority of their dour and reproachful gaze. Dixon gets a satisfaction from it that sickens him in his soul. In the dark cab of the car all he can see is her mouth painted full and dark with lipstick and the glowing white silk wrap, which he now lurches toward and tears from her head, pulling out a few hairs with it. Cate screams truncatedly and shrinks against the passenger door.

Dixon has the thing in his hands and does not know what to do with it. It suddenly seems like a living creature that he's mangled. He sets it down on the gearbox with a certain gentleness and ceremony.

He begins to speak, to say something, the form of which he has not yet decided, but the sight of Cate cowering against the door of the Buick stops him cold. The spectral hand closes on his throat again. He's a sissy once more. His clothes are pompous and his hair, slicked into that flawless helmet of comb-lines, is desperate. Look at him. Getting tough with a ninety-eight pound female. Chasing her into a corner like a beaten animal. The one person he could never bear to see him this way. And even now, her potency is undiminished. She is nine years old, tugging her socks up and touching her tongue to her nose. As he looks at her a calm steals over him. Even a type of happiness. He wants to tell her that he loves her. He wants to make her understand. He loves her more than life itself, because he doesn't love life very much at all.

"Get out of my car," he says.

Rounding the Mulholland Fountain, back in the city, Dixon rear-ends a Studebaker Champion and mutilates the fender. This is a part of town that he should not even be in, but his mind has wandered—did they find Cate's wayward brother in a brothel or a drug den, he wonders, or was his Jeep turned over in a ditch?—and he missed his turn by a couple of miles. He is lucky, though; the driver is a fan. Dixon gives him a hundred dollars and signs a cocktail napkin. The Buick is pristine. He feels a welling of affection for this dauntless piece of steel. He sits on the hood with his hands in the pockets of his natty gray trousers and watches the fountain jump. The penumbral glow of Los Angeles violates the night. It is summer and there never was a place with summer nights more brilliant and changeless than this.

Back home with a cigarette and a nightcap, the phone rings.

"You up, Dix? Hope it's not too late. I'm in London and I can't remember what the hell time it is back home."

"I'm up."

"Bad news. Can you handle a little bad news?"

"Is it about Frank Sinatra?"

"Why would it be?"

"I thought he might be mad."

"Mad at you?"

"I spoke out of turn, if you know what I mean." He laughs shakily.

"Dix, I don't know how to say this. Frank Sinatra doesn't know who the fuck you are. Anyway, it doesn't have a thing to do with him. The record company changed their minds, say they can't take a chance on a Spanish version. I don't know what to tell you. We're getting clobbered by Nashville and some of these nigger groups out of Detroit. Just hold on until the fad goes by. We'll be all right."

"Yeah, we'll be all right." Dixon has the white silk headwrap in his hand, turning it like a rosary. "Listen, I was thinking. Maybe we should talk to Capitol about a deal."

Hesitation on the other end. "Sure, Dix. We can talk to Capitol. Let 'em finish the building first, okay? Then we'll talk. And meanwhile, don't worry. These things come and go."

"Sure they do."

"You got class, Dix, and class is forever."

Night Drive

By Jason Katzenstein

They should pull people over for 'driving while introspective'. There's no way I'm fit to be on the road when I get in this mood.

I can't even listen to music. Not when music is meant to take the place of an obsessive, internal monologue.

I love music too much to use it as a soundtrack.

It gets foggy like this at 2 am, and I imagine that I'm living inside of a snow globe,

or some abandoned theater set.

When it gets bad I think about David Foster Wallace's short story, "Good Old Neon", where the already-dead narrator says, "One clue that there's something not quite real about sequential time the way you experience it is the various paradoxes of time supposedly passing and of a so-called 'present' that's always unrolling into the future and creating more and more past behind it. As if the present were this car—nice car by the way—and the past is the road we've just gone over, and the future is the headlit road up ahead we haven't yet gotten to, and time is the car's forward movement, and the precise present is the car's front bumper as it cuts through the fog of the future, so that it's now and then a tiny bit later a whole different now, etc. Except if time is really passing, how fast does it go? At what rate does the present change? See? Meaning if we use time to measure motion or rate—which we do, it's the only way you can—95 miles per hour, 70 heartbeats a minute, etc.—how are you supposed to measure the rate at which time moves? One second per second? It makes no sense. You can't even talk about time flowing or moving without hitting up against paradox right away...

...So think for a second: What if there's really no movement at all? What if this is all unfolding in the one flash you call the present, this first, infinitely tiny split-second of impact when the speeding car's front bumper's just starting to touch the abutment, just before the bumper crumples and displaces the front end and you go violently forward and the steering column comes back at your chest as if shot out of something enormous? Meaning that what if in fact this now is infinite and never really passes in the way your mind is supposedly wired to understand pass, so that not only your whole life but every single humanly conceivable way to describe and account for that life has time to flash like neon shaped into those connected cursive letters that businesses' signs and windows love so much to use through your mind all at once in the literally immeasurable instant between impact and death, just as you start forward to meet the wheel at a rate no belt ever made could restrain—THE END." Yeah, THE END of that story because the narrator kills himself in a car crash.

What if there is no movement? What if it's all like comics panels, a series of completely still images juxtaposed next to each other that we trick ourselves into seeing as contiguous? And at that point what's to stop you from making the same argument about meaning? That it's a necessary and retroactive imposition upon the dispassionate machinations of an indifferent universe?

Fuck, I need to park.

JASON KATZENSTEIN NIGHT DRIVE

There's this Presbyterian church on Mullholland that has a parking lot that's only ever used on Sundays.

On nights when I want to feel lonelier, I go there and look out at the city, and it's hard to tell where the lights end and the stars begin.

Like at the end of a movie when the camera zooms out until the hero becomes indistinguishable from everybody else walking down the street.

Or the last paragraph of The Dead.

"Yes, the newspapers were right: snow was general all over Ireland. It was falling softly upon the Bog of Allen and, further westwards, softly falling into the dark mutinous Shannon waves. It was falling too upon every part of the lonely churchyard where Michael Furey lay buried. It lay thickly drifted on the crooked crosses and headstones, on the spears of the little gate, on the barren thorns. His soul swooned slowly as he heard the snow falling faintly through the universe and faintly falling, like the descent of their last end, upon all the living and the dead."

Except snow is never general all over Los Angeles.

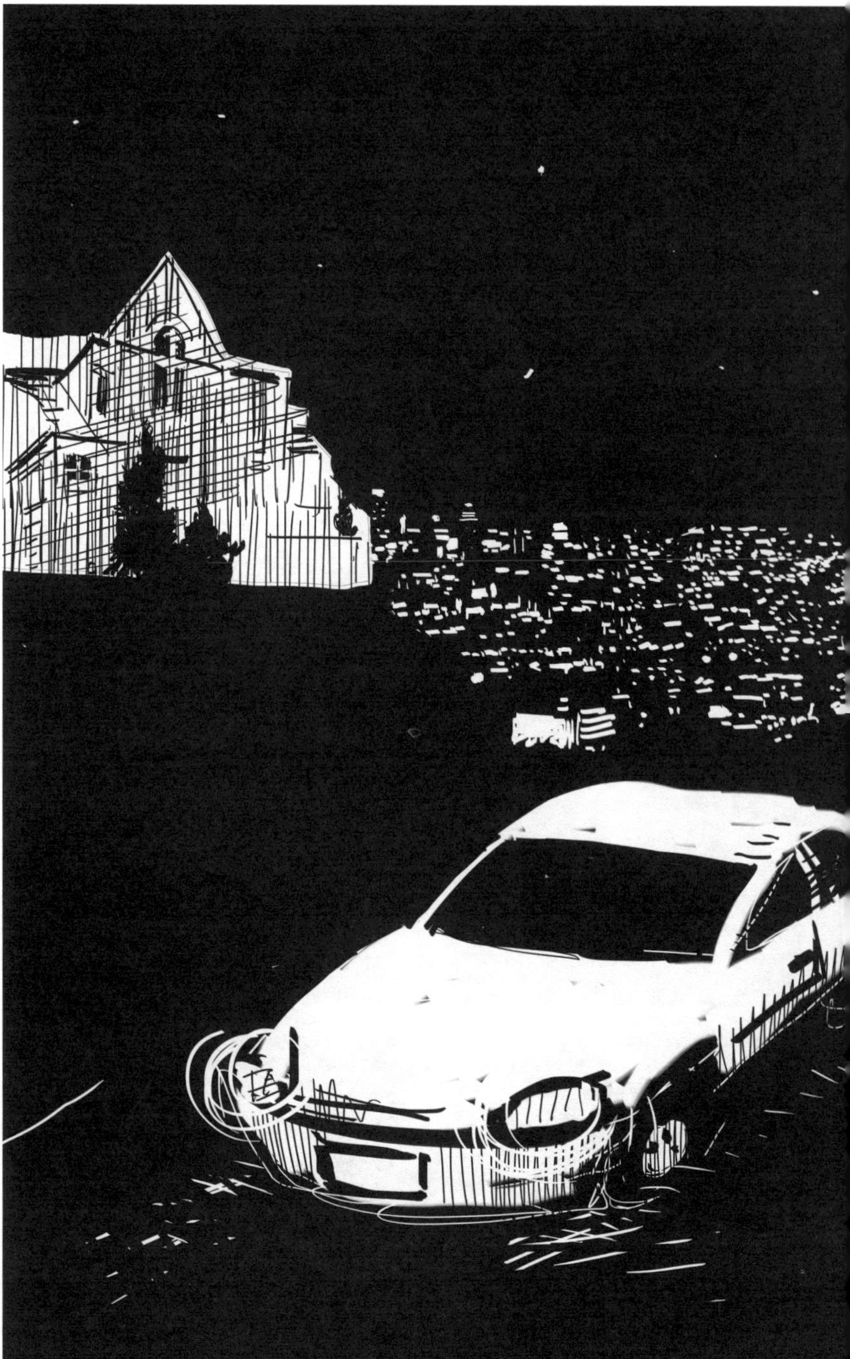

JASON KATZENSTEIN NIGHT DRIVE

Kim Vodicka

POD♥NK ANGST

You can't fall in love and live.

I got a problem.
It's called
I GET IT.

All day.
All blood.
Everyday.
Everybloody.

Rippin' the love bugs in two.

A lifeless ordinary.

Fabulosity malled over by dollface.

Doth neurosis without petals bloom?

I got anus hearts wazoo
in a shit brown colored mood.

Ew York Shitty.

Like a glass bottle of Heinz Tomato Ketchup,
all or nothin', baby.

When I piss and close my eyes feel sparkly.

When I piss so deep my soul is leaving me.

When my good god damn is winding down.

So slowly glows your radioactive cuntdown.

And so it goes your so especially meltdown.

Can't afford to not have the shakes.

Throwin' darts at the US map
tryin' to find where the party at.

Suiciety.

I cancelled my dismembership.

I want "Fuck All Y'all" tattooed on my fuckface.

Imps of the pervert.

Goin' down on herstory.

My vaginal means your button.

Two pinks talkin' the stink.

Scentsless roses r-r-revved upRAWR.

RealiT&A.

TampON&OFF.

Re♥ed.

This is a coming of age book for girls.

We work our way from the bottoms up.

Incriminated by virtue of ever having.

Thus the heavens cry subterfuge.

Oh, heavens!
To you!
Tonight!
I do!

Get it together.
Decompose yourself.

The rocking horse loser,
deceased without a cure,
and my partridge eyes just soar.

A butterfly landed on my mouth,
picked it off like a scab,
left me sore.

For love,
AC Slater that whore.

Matthew Socia

CONTEST

As a Midwesterner transplanted to the East Coast, I can tell you that there's a huge clot of people in lush CT who think everybody east of The Rockies and west of NYC spends their youth wading in seas of muck and corn. Sure, the Chicagoans are urbane in their own way, they say, but once you get past the city's tendrils, well, do they even have highways? A queenly woman tried to make small talk with me once, and asked whether one would have to boil Michigan water before drinking it. I run with this. Yes, I tell them. *Of course* you need to boil it, to avoid the cholera, which is an epidemic in rural Michigan. I tell them that the outhouse was nice, but it sure was a treat once we got the flusher. I conjure images of me, as a child, sidling past bear dens on my walk to school. I say sodie-pop, and they love it. They lick their East Coast chops, lean in, pearls dragging impolitely along the tabletop, and implore me to continue.

What I say is misleading, but not wholly untrue. Midwestern kids *do* do a great deal of teeth cutting in the woods. The first time you wander a little too far, a little too late, and you look through the shades of gray and orange as tree branches fractal in the fading sun, and you realize that you might become that child who never returned, is a pretty teachable moment. You get cut, and the way it bleeds convinces you this is it: your story, your final moments. And you lie there in the leaves for what must be hours, each breath your last, until you muster the will to drag yourself home, where Mom greets you at the door without word one of your bleeding arm, and you eat dinner with your family, quietly, never confessing that today you overcame death. This is the Midwest to me. Guess and checks in the deep forest paths, exploring and poking and overturning, each day a sine wave of succumbing and surmounting, alone through it all.

But I don't tell East Coast people this; I tell them about cowtipping and crystal. I tell them what they want to hear. And when they are totally rapt and salivating and I'm fully licensed to shock, I tell them about the night when, deep in the Northern Michigan forest, miles from it all, I grew up.

When I was seventeen, I was duped in public by my father and his friends. It happened in the heart of Michigan's wilderness, in a place so remote the term helicopter rescue might be used. There, each fall, in a carved out nook with two-tracks emanating in all directions, an unofficial Toughman contest is held. The official Toughman Contest is an amateur boxing championship known for being thoroughly hick and more than a bit brutal. It's already a bit of an institution in the Midwest, and is as legit as something like that can get, with doctors' notes, proof of age, etc. Toughman's cult rising, though, has caused several less bureaucratically rigorous copycats to rise from the murk, and it's to one of these deranged step-cousin tournaments that Dad dragged me that night.

East Coasters are creeped out by the idea of the Toughman Contest, but when I describe this one as unofficial, rules in it only suggestions, they literally recoil. It's then I tell them that as we blazed the back roads I saw meth labs set up like pit stops. This becomes just too much for them, and they reach their frog soft hands over to mine, as if to say, "Bless you for transcending all this." I agree with them; the whole thing is something that should have been evolutionarily molted by now, nothing I'd ever have considered attending. But Dad invited me in that way that wasn't really a question. "You want to go to a Toughman contest," he said, and I answered yes in the way I always did, which was to say nothing at all. Two hours later I was in a truck with two of his friends and their sons, rocking down uneven roads like they were rough seas.

There were six of us at the tournament: me and Dad, Dad's friend Buck and his son Bo, and some new guy whose name I never got, but whom I call Squirt Sr., because he referred to his pre-K aged son as Squirt, or, sometimes, My Lil' Squirt.

The facilities had the disheveled look of Christmas decorations in spring. The fight and beer tents were wine-red, the ground was caked and nearly bald, and I imagined that from above the whole place looked like a complex abscess.

We arrived near the end of the Toughwoman contest. In the ring was a fight between a chopstick of a woman with an eagle's nest of hair and a wobbly, pumpkin-shaped one. The heavier woman threw hammer punches without regard for defense or openings, marching at her opponent like a wind-up toy. The one who looked like she chose cigarettes over food did her best to impersonate a real boxer, weaving and dodging, pretending to look for openings. Dad had said in the truck he only wanted to catch the end of the Toughwoman contest, because it was "only funny for a lil' bit."

After the first round, Squirt had to go to the bathroom. The others decided I was the most suited to take the little tyke to the port-a-johns.

Squirt and I left as some teenage girl circled the ring in a bikini, holding a big black sign with FIGHT 2 rendered in white electrician's tape. On the way out, I picked up a fight schedule flyer from the usher at the main gate.

East Coast people don't get what I mean by the gray-green odor of portable carnival food stalls, the smell of fryer and fuel merging into a horrid, greasy fog you can taste and feel sticking to your face. Squirt and I walked the gauntlet, him pausing for a moment at the elephant ear stand to get a whiff.

As I waited outside the port-a-johns for Squirt, I read the fight schedule, and—here's the point in the story where I'm met with the most incredulity—on the list of fighters I saw my own name.

> Nick Friegle   168
> Phil Hommel   163
> Bobby 'The Flayer' Hughes 159

That was me, right down to the 163 I'd read on the scale after Dad said the school called and needed to know my weight for some forms, and... and then I put it together.

East Coasters ask me questions now. How could they sign you up without you knowing? No one would do that to their own son, their flesh and blood, would they? Weren't you underage? I answer by saying I don't know how or why it happened. My guess is that they wanted as many fighters as they could get. More fighters means more time patrons spend there, means more beer and corn dogs sold. And I could see an event organizer taking my Dad at his word that I was of age and willing. The CT people say words like injustice and abuse at this point, fussing with their pantsuits, chins wobbling with anger. I tell them it's not something to get worked up over because Midwesterners can be piteously ignorant. Yes, yes, I suppose they are, they say as they unclench.

I thought of taking off with Squirt. Five hours, I thought, would have been enough for my fight to come and go. If we hiked for a bit, played some games, he wouldn't even have known he was being kidnapped. I could have played dumb when we returned. Squirt Sr. probably was too drunk already to notice our disappearance. Lil' Squirt and I did a few laps around the perimeter of the grounds, hand in hand, while I toyed with abducting him.

Of course I didn't do it. We were back to our seats well before our absence became suspiciously long. As I slunk into my chair, anvil-headed Bo smiled at me like he had a secret. Bo was my age, and, according to my Dad, a child to be studied and emulated. He was easy to parody: snort a bit, sit so lazily it looks like you're holding an invisible boulder. He had spent the bulk of the car ride shadowboxing the seat in front of him.

We watched the women go at it; Dad said nothing about my forthcoming show, and I nothing to him. It would have been a show, I thought: a spectacle. I got a better look at my audience. The man in front of me was burly and dressed to be unapproachable. I saw a swastika tat's clapping hands peeking out from under his collar. The woman next to him wore a cropped leather jacket with occult patches, and had hair the texture of tinsel. She turned around once to face someone behind me, and smiled the most mind-searing tweaker's smile I've ever seen. A cluster of bikers howled like gorillas on the other side of the ring.

Later, as the Toughwoman finalists were hoisted into the ring, Dad turned to me and said, "Buck, why don't you and Phil go get some beers for the guys." Bo, Buck, and Squirt Sr. stared at me through wide smiles.

"Yes, let's," Buck said. He grabbed my shoulders, and we were off.

Buck didn't even pretend to do our task; we were walking toward Dad's truck, which was on the opposite side of the grounds from the beer tent. It was getting cold; I could see my breath. When we arrived he reached into the truck's bed, pulled out a hidden duffel bag, and chucked it to me. I let it hit my chest and fall to the dirt.

"Put this stuff on and meet me back at the registration table," he said, then walked toward the fight tent.

I opened the duffel bag and saw a mouth guard still in its package, boxing shorts with a dangling price tag. I went to the port-a-johns to get changed.

While putting the suit on in the chemical reek of the outhouse, I decided it would be best to rip the Band-Aid and fight. I could go in, dance around a bit, maybe throw some punches, take a quick fall and be out. No one gets *that* hurt doing it, I thought. No one dies.

CT people interject here. They tell me they remember seeing on the news that someone *did* die at an event like this, and that if you ask them, the whole Toughman idea is repugnant. They say my father should be ashamed not only for tricking me into fighting, but for even taking me.

After I finished putting on my costume, I reveled in my determination until the port-a-john suddenly lurched to the deep sound of quickly flexing plastic. Then again. Then several times in quick succession, like someone was going at its walls with a hammer. I went outside, where I saw a twenty-something guy with a mohawk punching the outhouse like it had called his mom a whore. His eyes widened and he began to emit a low, guttural shout with each strike. Then he stopped, turned toward me without acknowledgment, leaned back, pumped his arms, and howled.

I rescinded my earlier resolve. I was not tough. I was not a

Toughman. I'm still not tough nor a Toughman. I may have grown up with this type of Midwestern rubble, moistened my jowls with them, but I wasn't one of them, and I wasn't going to get clobbered by one for my Dad's amusement. I fled to the woods like a deer.

After a few tellings, I've found this is the best place to stage an intermission. I feign having to use the facilities, or I ask if anyone needs a tea refill, whatever it takes to get me out of the room. When I return, the average CT person doesn't inquire about my flight to the woods, but will redirect the story to my father.

Did he beat you, or worse, they ask. I tell them no, he didn't do anything like that to me. The best way I've found to express it is I always had the feeling that, given the choice and available technology, he would have refurbished me. I was pretty good, but not exactly what he signed up for. I give them morsels: Dad enrolling me in a masculinity boosting faux boot camp for preteens, and me pleading to deaf ears for my removal; a spiky fish having a plucked-from-water seizure on a boat's floor, and Dad calling me a wimp when I refused to touch it; the stage make-up story. Most are true, but I have a knack for improvising some tear-cranking whoppers.

When I get back to the story of me in the woods, I tell them how, at night, under the clear harmonics of the Northern Michigan fall sky, the forest takes on the qualities of a machine. There's a computerized whir as the breeze navigates the jutting topography. Branches rub each other, clicking like a clock being wound. The woods' moonlit pallor is the cold blue of metal. Then I really ladle it on, and say that I, smaller than the smallest gear's tooth, felt the crushing weight of the forest-machine, the immensity of it, and it felt near the same as my father's scorn, as he waited, smiling, for me to fail. I tell them I imagined my escape: me turned into some creature, disappearing into the mathematics of the forest. And I say other things just as gooey.

Again, what I tell them is not wholly true, because what *is* true is even more mawkish. That night, as I slowly shuffled down deer paths, I considered the cruel trajectory of my life. Fight or flight, I was going to be humiliated, and I saw myself in the future, failing and failing. The truth is I didn't give much thought to my father's treachery, but dwelt on how fleeing from it gave it credence. My life, I thought, would never be in my hands, but would stay clamped in this wooded Midwestern machine's grip, turning and jerking and meaningless. I looked through the forest night's infinite trigonometry, and succumbed.

In my boxer's getup, shivering like a crystal in the cold, I found a leafy clearing, and, wounded, laid down in it. I breathed slowly, my gloved hands looking like lobster claws, willing each moment to recede into no one's memory, and waited for my body's cells to freeze.

Offing oneself by hypothermia is obviously physically uncomfortable, but that night I noticed it was also really boring. It was too cold to sleep, and I couldn't burrow into anything or else I would have defeated my purpose. All I could do was lie there. Chalk it up to an American attention span, but I lost my will to have no will in minutes flat.

I loafed around a bit in the clearing, pretending to think about finding a river. I leaned, thug-like, on a nearby tree, a birch with old paint curls sloughing off, and peered through the thicket at the orange haze of the tournament. Dad and Squirt and the rest were there waiting for me, perhaps beginning to wonder if I was coming back.

I had a moment then. Not an epiphany or anything dramatic, but a moment for sure. It was that feeling like when you look at your room and it's a mess, and you decide that today it gets cleaned, and you clean it, and you feel on a roll, so you make a cleaning schedule for, like, two years, and *this* time you'll commit to the schedule, and you still have this life-sorting antsiness after that, so you get all your bills in order, and decide what you're going to do with yourself career-wise for the rest of your life, and then you sit back and bask in your productivity. What I decided that night in the woods was that I wasn't going to be concerned anymore with what anyone made of me. It's a totally insipid thing to say, something they've been drilling into us since self-esteem classes dipped their beaks into the schools' curricula, but there you have it. Under the duress of having to fight in front of a bunch of loathsome rednecks, I became mysteriously Zen-like. I realized I didn't care if I got up in that ring and acted like a jackass in front of those loathsome rednecks. In fact, I relished the idea of it. I wanted to get in that ring and prance for them, caper in ways those hillbillies had only seen on their friends' cable.

I made my way back to the ring for my call.

As I approached the grounds, the tournament's features came into focus. I noticed how sylvan the whole place was, as if it had been whittled instead of set up. The figures, as they scooted about, were shadowy and deft, like elves or druids. When I saw a young, prematurely bald man vomiting near the port-a-johns, spinning wildly as he did so, this image collapsed. The man flopped to the ground to the laughter of his buddies. I arched way clear of them and retrieved my bag of street clothes from the port-a-john I had changed in.

Registration was near the beer tent. When I arrived, I saw a crowd of men in a cordoned off square filled with standing punching bags. The men looked furious, frowning, huffing through their noses. They hit the punching bags as hard as they could over and over, some with running starts. A man in the back kept doing jump spin kicks that surely wouldn't be effective in the ring, but would have looked nice on film. Sitting at a nearby table was another man who, aside from all the flannel, looked like he could have been a politician.

"Phil Hommel checking in to fight."

"You're fighting?"

"Yes. Phil Hommel."

"Hommel…Hommel… Geez, kid, you're on next. Know the rules?"

"Yes."

"One kick per round. Trainer can't enter the ring. Where's your trainer?"

I popped in my mouth guard, shrugged, then ran to the ring.

I *had* really made it just in time; moments after getting to ringside, I watched a man crumple like a shot doe to the roar of the audience. The victor and the ref dragged the loser out of the ring. The girl in the bikini walked by with a sign that said FIGHT 12. I did a stylish vault over the ropes, which got a few hoots and hollers.

I thought I'd tower over everyone like a titan once I was in the ring, but not so. The audience seemed at eye level, and with that many eyes focused on me, I felt tiny. The ring itself was not as big as I predicted, cramped almost. I found Dad and his friends poking their heads up from behind the massive guy with the unsavory tat.

The ref hopped back into the ring and said through the sound system: "Ladies and gentleman, we've got one fighter and one coward, so let's give a hand to our round 12 winner…" He covered his mike, leaned close to me, and asked, "What's your name, kid?"

"Phil Hommel."

"PHIL HOMMEL!"

The ref lifted my arm then whispered, "Go tell Ricky what happened."

There was some polite clamor, nothing like the end of FIGHT 11. I guessed Ricky was the politician in country boy clothes who had registered me. I went back to see him.

CT people look disappointed here; they all hope for bloodshed, my transcending my father's scheme through some sportsman apotheosis, and, after my victory, him crying at my feet for forgiveness. They want a KO followed by a vacuum silence, and then a crowd in such a fit of hysterics that its wispiest members faint. Indeed, if it looks like their Midwest fascination is wearing thin, or if I just can't stomach another sip of their locally grown tea, I give them that ending and skedaddle. For the rest, I drudge on. And what the rest forget, and I, in my preoccupation with the victory, also forgot, was that this was a tournament.

"You'll get a bye to the next round, cause your opponent wussed out," Ricky told me.

"I'm not done?"

47

"No, boy, you're one step closer to the trophy."
"Is my fight far off?"
"Looks like a good four fights until your round comes up again."
"So...?"
"Thirty minutes, plus or minus."

For the third time that night I accepted I was going to have to brawl. The first time I accepted it to get it over and done, then to mock my father's trick, but this time I was in it to pummel. After being in the ring and feeling the rush of all-eyes-on-me, I wanted to wallop someone and really get the crowd going. I went to the pen to tidy up my form.

There were more men than punching bags, about two to three per. As I maneuvered the frenetic maze, I noticed there was a tacit rule system. About a minute a person per bag. From a bit of eavesdropping, I inferred that while it was first come first serve, there was a bit of bag time precedence for those on deck. Only give advice when asked. Keep personal distance. It seemed rather organized once I poked around in its veins. I queued up.

The man in front of me was practicing what I knew to be uppercuts. He would do a ghost-sparring dance, dodge some imaginary, poorly timed punch, and sock the bag in its nonexistent chin. I noticed he had some seriously sturdy gams that could easily deliver a knockout kick. When he finished, he queued right up again behind me.

Boxing works its way into enough movies that I knew the basic forms and punches, but not their names. When I got to the bag I recalled those scenes, and did what I'd seen actors do. I practiced a left right double hit, a satisfyingly rhythmic combo I registered as what people meant by a one-two. I did this weird number that looked like riding a bike in place, each push of the pedal coinciding with a punch. I weaved in and did a strong right hand to the bag's gut. The sound for that one was more addicting than the physicality of it; when I hit it in just the right spot, there was a thwack like beating a rug with a tennis racket.

The man and I traded off a few times before he broke one of the pen's rules.

"Keep your hands up," he told me. "You can't defend with them down, and you'll be quicker to counter."

"Like this?" I asked, and brought them up to my face.

"More like this." He torqued my palms to face each other. "And punch like each punch is going to be a KO. Commit."

He punched the bag's imaginary midsection with a flourish no one would have allowed time for in a real fight, and made the customary *psh* sound that all these guys must have learned from each other. In the pen, it sounded like a distant waterfall, with all the white fuzz *psh*'s and bag thwacks. I appeased the guy and punched the bag.

"No. Commit. You have to commit, kid. Rule numero one," he punched again, and the bag tottered like a drunk. I hit it another time.

"This is... What are you doing? Are you in this to win?"

"Of course I am," I said, then remembering his advice was unsolicited. I punched as hard as I thought I could.

"What I'm seeing is a lack of committal. To succeed, each moment you need to decide and do, decide and do, both, constantly, without flinching. Decide to punch and punch. You could connect, or an invisible hook could crack your pretty little temple, and you're a smear on the ring's floor. Commit to failure or success."

"But I'm not a –"

"It's convincing yourself you'll do something versus actually doing it."

The man couldn't have been much older than me. Early twenties, maybe. He had an outdated mustache, and camouflage shorts. He waited for my response with his gloved hands on his hips.

I heard my name through the pen's din. "HOMMEL! HUGHES!" Ricky called from the registration table. I left my impromptu lesson.

At the registration table, I saw the mohawked guy who disturbed me in the outhouse. Ricky said, "You two are on next. The one going on now is a pretty lopsided fight, should be over quick. Wait by ringside." We walked single file into the tent.

The fight was already over when we arrived; the boxers were exiting the ring. A new woman, an older blonde with crossed eyes and legs up to here, stomped around the ring's edge holding a FIGHT 18 sign. My opponent, I noticed as he slid into the ring like a seal, wasn't all that strong-looking. His back looked baby soft, and he had chicken legs. I hopped into the ring like before.

"In this corner, weighing 159 pounds, BOBBY 'THE FLAYER' HUGHES! And in this corner, weighing 163 pounds, PHIL HOMMEL!"

I remember thinking how exactly like a television show our intros were, and that comparison continued as we popped in our mouth guards and walked around the ring with our gloves raised for all to see. In my tour, I saw Dad and co. standing, Squirt draped sleeping over Bo's shoulder. Dad made a give-'em-hell air punch. Squirt Sr. was bent over. Buck was lighting up.

The ref ushered us to our corners. The Flayer did these weird coffee grinder sweep kicks, maybe designed to intimidate. I did some shadowboxing in my corner, spinning around, imagining a hooded cape draped over my head. The bell sounded.

No one I've told this to has been in a fight, either organized or off the cuff. You're in the ring and all you can do is think about knocking out that mohawked form in front of you, and you know he only wants to knock you out, and the world is a flutter of choice followed by choice. Anxiety hollows you to a dodging and choosing husk, light as air. East Coast people usually patronize me and say something like "boxing's a sport steeped in history," whatever that means. I'm not attached to the sport itself, or the idea of Toughman, and I think a lot of the CT people think I'm justifying it, despite all the negative press I relay. That moment, though, Toughman showed me that even way out in the forest, in the podunkiest of places, under the glare of an audience praying for my demise, I could decide and do.

I danced toward my opponent, and he toward me. He paused, and I saw my opening. My fist pounced at his exposed cheek, but just as I was about to hit, as I flirted with triumph, I saw the peach blur of his leg as his thresher kick connected. A perfect counter. His foot cracked me in the skull, and, I'm told, I spun around four times before actually landing prone on the mat.

I remember getting pulled from the ring, but then nothing until I was sitting back in the stands with Dad and his buddies. My left eye was fused shut, and my view through the other one was blurry. The men seemed surprised I went through with the fight, a bit proud of me, and not terribly concerned I had failed so spectacularly. Bo wanted to know what it felt like to be kicked; I never told him. Squirt Sr. kept asking me what happened to my face. Dad didn't really say anything. I put my head in his lap, and laid across a few chairs. He didn't push me off.

A good fifteen minutes later, I looked up from my Dad's lap at the looming bottom half of his face. My head throbbed. I wasn't angry at him anymore, just sad. Sad that I knew I was going to have to make choices that I knew to be my own, choices I knew would slowly separate us as we grew older.

"Dad?" I said.
"Hmm?"
"Dad."
"What is it?"
"I know what I want for my next birthday."
"What's that?"
"A dress."
"Phil..."
"Red. Size 6."
"I..."

Buck looked over at me then gave my Dad the raised eyebrow. I pushed it.

"Two dresses!" I yelled. "I want two dresses!"

The man with the tat stirred in his seat. Dad looked worried. I smiled.

I like to remain cagey about that last part when I tell this story. The CT people get up, stretch, and say, as casually as they can, So does that mean, you know... I tell them no, I didn't get the dresses. They look like they want to ask something else, and I say Dad still lives in Michigan.

What I usually tell them at the end is that on our way out of the tournament, I noticed how oddly calming it is to drive down backwoods roads, especially at night. The way the turns doppler to dark nowhere. The sweeping sound of the grass on the truck's undercarriage. In fall, the trees become tall skeleton hands with overlong fingers, looking almost alien in the headlights. That night, I watched the trees' fingers clasp above us, and the longer we drove, the more the woods seemed like a cathedral in shape and demeanor.

Squirt, somehow, was able to stay asleep despite all the turbulence. He sat next to me, his head tucked into the crook of his dad's arm. I imagined him in just that position someday, contemplating his own fate deep in the forest, sprawled over leaves, his head resting on some stump, waiting, as I'd done, for life to occur.

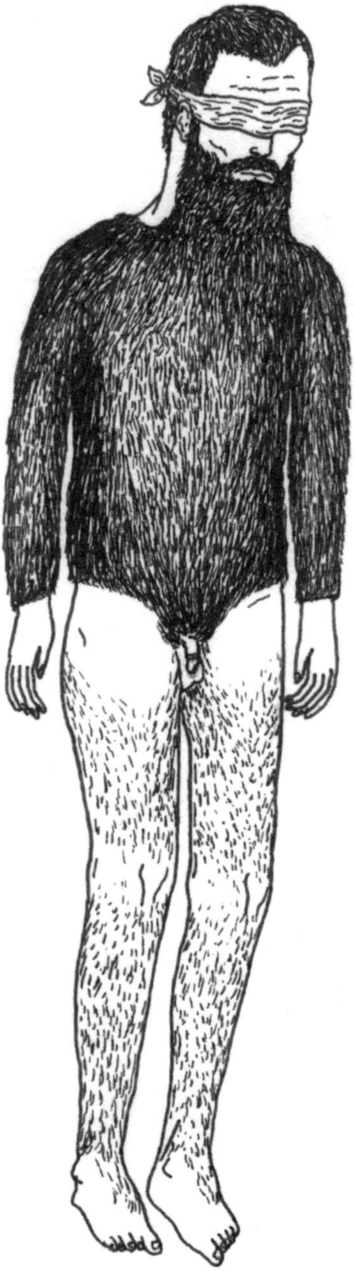

Kelin Loe

from **TOXCIN TOCSIN! OR THE ORIGINS OF KELIN LOE!**

Light switch imagery did not help me understand the penis. I believed them to be either up or down.

And I believed up was only perpendicular, the sheet tent from that movie with Josh Hartnett.

I was in my day bed, and my cousins were in sleeping bags. Bethany told a story of an intruder. In the mirror, my aunt saw two feet under the shower curtain.

That a penis has a spectrum of motion means it is not a hammer.

MISSISSIPPI is the first major hangman word for many Minnesotan children.

We decided that, in the event of an intruder, the bathroom was the safest place for children.

Just then a shadow knocked at my basement window. Natalie threw Bethany to the floor as they made for the bathroom.

I ran to tell my parents and aborted and pounded the bathroom door.

The figure moved through the open front door and it was my dad and that was the first time I wet my pants.

The first time I lived in a frat house, Charlie, I was in love with him, said: "You look like the type of person who falls down a lot."

I say, WHAT THE FUCK DOES THAT MEAN?

I found my parents in the dark family room watching the nightly news. I was three, the story I heard was about a babysitter. The baby was dying slowly in its crib while she was watching TV.

A shadow man knocked on the door. He told her the baby was dying, so she let him in.

The babysitter was saying how lucky she was on the news.

He went back to the baby's room, reached his arm into the baby's throat and pulled a locket out.

I just took a burning and fragrant shit in a bathroom scented cinnamon and washed my hands with mango soup.

The first time I shit my pants was in a nice pair of Gap underwear.

I thought I could hold it in.

I am about to lose my focus.

And I say, PERHAPS I LOOSE MY FOCUS.

The psychologist lays in front of me a wooden plank with holes and teaches me to stack pegs.

I am timed.

I SAID, I AM TIME.

I saw a large turtle pulling towards the highway.

IF YOU ARE ABOUT TO KILL YOURSELF, ARE YOU DYING?

My husband and I are so small that we fit perfectly in the nineteenth century homes we tour.

Am I better off to myself dead or alive?

DEAD.

Poetry.

Am I better off to my husband dead or alive?

ALWAYS ALIVE.

Until once.

When I was little I thought that anything big enough to get lodged in the throat was a cause of death.

After a fight with my mother, I held a bouncy ball on my tongue, pumping myself up to swallow.

But I would not die by ball.

It was salty and sort of chewy. THAT SOUNDS NICE AND HUMAN, but it smelled like plastic.

It felt good to spit out.

It feels good to fall out.

I have been dying on the highway.

TO DIE WOULD NOT BE TO FALL OUT.

I want to know what the opposite of a fall is.

I do not want to KNOW the opposite of a fall.

The first time I saved a life, my mom was working on dinner, and my little brother was in his high chair. His arms flapped hands loose, his mouth open and chest still.

I AM A SHADOW MAN.

AND I FELL OUT.

AND I FELL OUT A SHADOW MAN.

(I FELL OUT OF A SHADOW MAN.
AND I FELL OUT AS A SHADOW MAN).

I screamed that he was choking, and my mom rushed over, and put her pinkie in his throat and pulled a carrot out. He cried for a while and vomited white foam across the table.

I AM AN EMETOPHOBE.

This whole fucking thing is a board game about staying alive.

Andrew Durbin

WARM LEATHERETTE

I

Lil Wayne ruined death.

In spring 2013, the rapper near-fatally overdosed on medicinally-infused sizzurp, an hallucinogenic mixture of fruit soda and cough syrup, fortified with codeine and promethazine, seized up on stage and shook in his leopard-print tights till near electric departure from stage and world, was rushed to the hospital and emerged alive, but not before nearly disappearing forever into a fizzy, pharmaceutical haze.

Lil Wayne's hyperbolic single "Love Me" describes women as the agents of disappearance. The song not only privileges the male subject position in the various strata of intercourse, it valorizes the female as the necessary yet problematic participant that disrupts intercourse by her intervening consciousness of the activity. The female is an amnesiac object and the lush principle of silence that enables Lil Wayne to proceed in the bliss of unthinking until he comes and forcibly "comes to his senses," at which point he abstracts the woman to the multitude of frictive figures who oppose his streamlined administration of a better life. His bitches who love him obliterate his own need to maintain absence of responsibility with regard to the milieu of differing relationships that constitute his socio-sexual life like thunder storms that briefly ruin a summer day. It's only when they actively engage that he returns to himself, to everything, and sizzurp in the AM.

Women ruined the return. In summer 2008, two NYPD officers accompanied an intoxicated East Village woman leaving a bar to her home. They entered her apartment with her, left, and returned several times throughout the night to rape her while she passed in and out of consciousness. She sued the NYPD, but the court did not find the surveillance tapes that showed the police officers entering and leaving her home multiple times nor her testimony sufficient cause to convict the two men of rape. The NYPD dismissed the cops nevertheless in an effort to placate the mounting tensions between it and the public it "serves and protects." Shortly thereafter, the two police officers left the city, the woman disappeared, and I was detained in Fort Greene after I asked the police officer who had stopped me for an open container violation why he wasn't in the East Village raping women. He arrested me immediately.

Pressure ruined procedure. Ten years after 9/11, the NYPD conducted numerous illegal operations against the occupiers camped near the site of the World Trade Center. I think you might remember this time, when we stood together in general assembly for hours and, later, waited for free pizza. What was at first a simple act of communalization became the far more mysterious idea, lurking around us, of the possible futures shooting up from the ground everywhere to form or demolish prisons, depending on your perspective. The NYPD dragged the protesters from their tents and into the winter. During the next year the charges against the students, teachers, union workers, homeless, and others were dropped by the overburdened courts due to insufficient evidence to convict "the offenders." Fuck the police became such an illuminating mantra almost anyone could be heard saying in their sleep.

The overburdened ruined system. The poet Joan Retallack's poem "A I D / I / S A P P E A R A N C E" makes language disappear in a procedure that virally decomposes the found jargon of scientific inquiry, mimicking the fracturing of the body's defensive mechanisms by the AIDS virus. One time, I had tea with a friend my age living with HIV, much rarer these days, and he told he was struggling, over tea he was looking at me while a fire engine got stuck in traffic and

he said, though I could hardly hear him, he was struggling
with, with. Rivulets of clouds formed in the sky above us.
It is never summer anymore, it is only the eroded time
of normative climate patterns that once invisibly marked
and coordinated our development as individuals
until they were abstracted then removed and their absence
became a sudden, intense visibility in every day life. I was
sitting in the café, reading a poem by Joan Retallack, while
Lil Wayne's "Love Me" played loudly enough in someone
else's headphones that I could hear it several chairs away
and I thought (forgetting what my friend was struggling
with), this song sums up some degraded feeling of the
promoted self, jet set and breeze in the mix of medicinal
waste, all to get the fuck back, as Lawrence Giffin put it,
into that burning (private) plane.

My private plane is grounded in jargon. In an extract of a
paper on Retallack's poem, Bryan Walpert writes "Retallack
uses two connected lines of the postmodern critique of
science—linguistic slippage and paradigm-dependency—
not to subvert or to critique science as an end in itself but to
return," summer in spring
winter in fall
spring in winter
fall in summer,
"but to return,"
spring in summer
fall in winter
winter in spring
summer in fall
"but to return attention to the human subject, specifically in
the context of AIDS,"
fall in winter
spring in summer
summer in fall
winter in spring
"but to return" to the plane that has been set on fire by
Lil Wayne's retinue of sociopaths (a celebrity is someone
who desires to tell a joke that ends in the death
of the entire world external to himself/herself) after they
poured sizzurp all over the aisle seats and dropped matches
onto the soaked leather.

2

You could say that by this point the night's advanced
state of decomposition sufficiently illuminated
the flaming jet, which the local fire department could not
put out. We stood by the runway, near the tall security
fence, and drank Four Loko as the cool breeze forged
through the heat at midnight some better world we briefly
encountered, we being the numerous Facebook friends I've
never met but imagine might join me at this moment, who
have written messages to say a variety of interesting, sexy,
and also stupid things about me, my poetry, my friends,
what I can give them, and what they can give me. Love
me, I'd say. The moon never fails to surprise me when it
doesn't crash into us. The moon ruined the night.

Facebook ruined anonymity. To return to my friend in
summer, which was a kind of spring, he was telling me he
was struggling with paying his bills while remaining an
artist. What's become a cliché reverts to a very powerful
reality when it's married to economics, and if I could throw
a few fundraisers for him I would. We both have no money
and as long as we've known each other (almost ten years)
that has been the case. When we first met he was addicted
to crystal meth and loved volcanoes. He struck me as an
entirely original person who would go much "further in
life" than me, into and scaled by whatever indices of
success, progress, and attention art could offer him
in ten years. We didn't know that volcanoes have a
paradoxical affect on their environments, temporarily
deadening life and disrupting fragile underwater
ecosystems after they erupt, only to late become
a hotbed of life, and returns with more force than before.

Sometimes volcanoes ruin seasons. In 1816, the eruption of
Mount Tambora eliminated that year's summer, resulting
in very cold temperatures for June, July, and August,
as well as reduced crop yields, increased sickness, and
general malaise. In July 1816 "incessant rainfall" during
that "wet, ungenial summer" forced Mary Shelley, John
William Polidori, Lord Byron, and Percy Shelly to stay
indoors for much of their Swiss holiday. They decided to
have a contest to see who could write the best horror story,

leading Shelley to write *Frankenstein, or The Modern Prometheus* and Lord Byron to write "A Fragment," which Polidori later stole and rewrote as *The Vampyre*— a precursor to Dracula. Lord Byron was inspired to write a poem, "Darkness," at the same time. Those days were like a magic show, each manipulating out of their occupants curious events in literature that created entirely new acts of expression via the arrival and dismissal of certain ideas they harbored about one another. Dracula ruined horror, but not before betraying his first author by finding another. That summer killed many Europeans, none of whom could be stitched back into life by Dr. Frankenstein.

3

According to Wikipedia, the last member of any species is called an endling. The entry names five individuals who occupied this final slot in their respective evolutionary chains: Martha, Incas, Booming Ben, Benjamin, Lonesome George. Recently, I've started to say their names to myself before I go to bed, chanting and re-chanting them like a nursery rhyme: Martha Incas / Booming Ben / Lone-some George / and Ben-ja-min.

Tim writes to me to say that an endling triumphs over death because they are literally the death of the death of the species. When they disappear or are stuffed and mounted in the Smithsonian in Washington, D.C., they take with them the demise of everyone who might have survived them. I feel love for these endlings, and hope that love within its power can restore them to a kind of life. LOL. It is love, I think, that allows the future to finally emerge out of linear time in order to bring us back to the starting point. LOL. Love is an engine that reroutes the disappeared and returns them to their rightful place in the hierarchy of things we've lost but will soon reappear in the present more powerfully alive than before. LOL.

Repeat yourself a few times, say goodbye, listen to Selena Gomez, look at Tumblr, take a shower, read the news, read that Lil Wayne has been hospitalized, say goodbye, love me.

Repeat yourself a few times, read Dennis Cooper, text a
friend, go home, say goodbye, drink coffee, buy a chair,
listen to Selena Gomez, look at Tumblr, say goodbye, go to
bed, wake up in the middle of the night, say goodbye, listen
to Selena Gomez, look at Wikipedia, read the endlings,
say goodbye, love me.

Selena Gomez's "Naturally" is a counterpoint to Lil
Wayne's "Love Me" in its radical affirmation of the other
as an animating agent within the self and suggests a status
update in terms of the relationship between her and the
subject of love. I stand on the roof of my apartment on Park
Place and Nostrand Avenue, looking at Crown Heights in
early spring, waiting for the rain promised by my weather
app, listening to her unravel the logic of pure, scattering
desire via the voice of another, which she internalizes to
express in her own stunning hit the maximizing effect
of listening to someone you love speak, a voice we do not
hear that invigorates its listener. "How you choose to express
yourself, it's all your own, I can tell it comes naturally."
The act of speaking as one would normally speak takes
her breath away, supernaturalizing her romance into the
compatible forces of thunder and lightning. She is nature.
Pink sheets, skies fluttering, summer, shades drawn, lava
lamp, purple light, server crash, shared indices of faces
and bodies, Martha, hands between thighs, lips, lip-gloss,
Benjamin, Incas, AIDS, smoking weed, Lonesome George,
islands in the dark, Booming Ben, flash drive, sleep
well, cab ride, goodnight, forever forever forever, it comes
naturally.

Lydia Conklin

POM POM IS LOOSE

What?
I'm calling the pound in about two seconds!
Even though Pom Pom's dumb, it would be sad if she were in the pound.
Really sad.

Paul Crenshaw

BLIND DATE

"You blog?" he said. "As in, you have a regular blog-thing?"
"Yes," she said. "A blog-thing."
"As in, you do it every day? You're a blogger?"
"Yes. And yes."

She stirred her coffee. He felt the need to cross his legs. He rested one arm on the back of the painted wooden chair. On the yellow walls hung paintings from local artists you could buy for the price of a good hotel room or a great bottle of wine. Out the big windows people hurried toward buildings.

"About what?"
"Being a mother."
He paused with his hand on a sugar packet. "You have kids?"
"No."
"So you write a mommy-blog-thing without being a mother?"
"I offer advice on how to be a better mother. I don't claim I am one. And it's not a 'blog-thing.'"
He tapped the sugar packet on the table. "Sorry. I am not familiar with the terminology of writing stuff down and then calling it published."
"I don't call it published. I call it a blog."

He found himself wondering about her hygiene—shaved pits, or no? She seemed like the type who might forget deodorant for weeks at a time, especially in summer. "Isn't that a bit dishonest?"
"I just said—"
"Not that. Writing a 'mommy-blog' without being a mother."
She paused with the coffee cup at her mouth. "Why do you say 'mommy-blog' that way?"
He picked a piece of lint off his pants, smiling to himself. "No reason."

She looked everywhere around the room except at him. He could tell she bought her clothing at vintage stores. He wondered how many times she had caught lice. He had a feeling her breath would smell like

Mountain Dew. He imagined her desk littered with empty cans, flies crawling around the rims, her sitting in sweat pants and torn t-shirt.

"But that's your job?"

"That and other freelance opportunities I've gotten from my blog. Technical manuals. Food articles. Interviews."

He raised one eyebrow. "And you make a living at this?"

She had the feeling he raised his eyebrow a lot. Like whatever job he held had a weekly professional development program devoted to eyebrow raising—right height, right amount of skepticism, etc. "You already asked that. Three times. Is it so hard for you to believe? It's writing. I am a writer. People enjoy my work. What do you do?"

"I'm a financial advisor."

"Advisor?"

He inspected his fingernails. She could see he was a man who spent a lot of time on his fingernails. "Evaluation of portfolios, advice on recent market trends, analysis of long-term bonds and securities, etc."

"But you aren't actually a broker, you just advise people? And then they go to a broker?"

He looked briefly at the ceiling. He knew he had pissed her off and now she was trying to get back at him by making fun of what he did, blah-blah-blah. He was already bored, wished he never would have agreed to meet her. Fuck Ann, he thought, for setting us up. "That's what a financial advisor does."

"So you say, basically, 'Just pay me some money, I'll tell you what to do, and I have no responsibility after that'?"

"I suppose, if you want to use laymen's terms."

"Laymen's terms," she said to the ceiling. She imagined him bent over the IQ test in *Reader's Digest*, frowning at his score, changing a few answers. "And people trust you?"

"A lot of people trust me."

"Why?"

He had been looking at his watch, lifting the sleeve of his shirt enough to see the face, calculating how long he needed to sit here before he could safely leave. "Excuse me?"

"I said why? Why would people do that? Go to a total stranger for financial advice?"

"Isn't that exactly what you do? Give mommy advice, except you don't even have the expertise to shovel the shit you're shoveling."

Her smile looked like a coiled snake. "I don't claim to be an expert. You do. You have the big gold watch and the reassuring tie and the once-a-week haircut."

He raised the eyebrow again, this time in mockery, she was sure. "You write a blog. How is that a job?"

Her face had turned a shade of red he'd once seen in a living room. He could feel his ears getting hot. She said, "You take other people's money. You don't have anything at stake, and you don't actually do anything."

"Do you even get paid? Who pays you? Who reads your blog about mommy-food-arts-and-crafts or whatever the hell it is and says 'This person needs to be paid for this'?"

"How much do you skim off the top? What kind of kickbacks do you get from stock companies to give people false investment advice? Oh, don't tell me—I bet you're one of the 'honest' ones, the ones who 'take care of their customers' and really 'care about them' like they're 'family.'"

People were looking at them now. The espresso machine came on, loud in the sudden quiet. After a moment the low conversations began again, the soft clack of laptop keyboards, the clank of spoons stirring. He picked up his coffee and set it down. Great job, Ann, you bitch, he thought. Been sitting with this woman for less than ten minutes and we already hate each other. Great job of "finding someone who thinks like I do."

"I don't know why I even came here," he said to his fingernails. "I hate coffee shops. I hate blind dates."

"I do too."

She was on the verge of crying, he thought, but was too tough to let herself. She was not attractive, not classically attractive, anyway, no golden triangle perfect face, no mathematical formulas, no cream-condensers and all-day spas like his clients' wives used trying to stave off the ravages of time. But she had dropped the thin film people wear around themselves and he decided maybe she was like him a little bit. He put his leg down and leaned forward, trying to ignore his pulse.

He said, "Look, I'm sorry. I don't talk to people often. I guess I'm out of practice. I meet clients once, maybe twice, usually old couples who have spent their entire lives paying off their debts and now are ready to retire and I look at what they give me and want to tell them it's too late. That I can't do anything with what they have. I want to tell them to move into a rent-controlled apartment and learn to be happy with driving two hours to take a walk on the beach because they can't afford to live near one. And be happy with that two hour drive, because they can't afford to travel. Not if they live past seventy. If you die before you hit seventy, I want to say, then maybe you can afford a time-share in

Miami and to go to Europe a couple of times, but if you live any longer, you're fucked.

"But you can't say that. So I tell them to put their money in the highest-yield, lowest-risk market I can find, and when they get their statements each month they are happy. I mean, I guess they are. They don't come back, is what I'm saying. If they need to talk, they email me. They used to call, but they don't even do that anymore. I spend half my day answering emails. I hate emails."

She picked up her coffee cup then realized it was empty. People were still occasionally looking at them from the corners of their eyes, but mostly everyone had gone back to what they had been doing.

"I never talk to anyone," she said. "I guess that's why I came today. That, and the way Ann always looks at me. Like I am wasting my life without a husband. She starts sentences with 'My husband.' 'My husband tore his rotator cup playing tennis. My husband just finished that book and said it was even better than the movie. My husband—'"

"—is a drunken louse who beats me and writes fake prescriptions for Vicodin, but I feel better acting as if he is wonderful," he said in a good imitation of Ann's voice.

She snorted so loudly everyone looked at them again. She covered her mouth. She thought if she had had coffee in her mouth it would have gone all over him, and that made her laugh harder. She was pointing at him as if he had answered a charade correctly.

"Yes," she said. "Yes. That's it. It makes me feel creepy, like she may be hiding something."

"I get the same feeling from her. Like they have a trapeze in the bedroom, and some night they will have to call the ambulance to get the bedpost out of his ass."

She snorted again, even louder. A woman nearby looked at her, and she stared back until the woman looked away.

"Some of the people who respond on my blog strike me the same way. 'Thanks for the advice,' they say, all capital letters and eighteen exclamation points, as if me telling them it's ok to cut the umbilical cord before the kid hits twenty-one is sage advice. They even say things like 'YOUR ADVICE SAVED MY LIFE, OMG OMG OMG.' I think, what the hell are you talking about? How have I done anything for you? How are you that stupid?"

"These old people," he said. "They have no idea how they've wasted their lives. If they had started saving when they were young they'd be millionaires now. But they didn't. And the young couples don't come in because they're ass-deep in college debt. I want to scream at these old fucks, 'Hey, why didn't you think of retirement before, you know, you fucking retired.' They come waddling through the door in cheap clothes, with bad haircuts and front-butts and expect me to save them."

"Sometimes I get emails asking for advice. Usually love advice. Or framed as love advice. Like 'What should I cook him for a first dinner if I really want to impress him.' I should say 'Lady, if you really want to impress him, go down on him. If you want to have dinner, take him to a restaurant. Other than that, leave me alone.'"

"My last clients—this morning, actually—had twelve thousand dollars saved. They were both sixty-seven. Twelve thousand dollars. And the woman said 'We'd like to retire to Bermuda.' I wanted to tell her the only Bermuda she was retiring to was the Bermuda Triangle."

The lunch crowd was thinning out as it got to be afternoon. She had her elbows propped on the table. She didn't think he was really all that bad looking. His face was slightly oversized and he had a fake tan, but she had seen worse.

"Some people will respond to a blog a dozen times. Like, they'll sit there watching to see when someone else responds, and then agree with that person. They'll say 'I couldn't agree more' exclamation point exclamation point exclamation point. I think, How sad is your life?"

"Most people's lives are sad, if you think about it. Or disgusting."

The waitress came by carrying the coffee pot but she didn't stop. The woman put both hands around her cup to see if it had any warmth left. "You were right," she said. "About my blog. About any blog. It's just a place for people to feel as if other people are listening to them. It's a sad thing, how empty people are. All of us."

There were less people walking past the windows. The espresso machine came on again. In the back someone was talking on a cell phone.

"At least you never start sentences with 'My husband,'" he said.

She smiled but it didn't go all the way through. She nodded toward the cell phone talker. "Or do that." She smiled again, and this time made it to mischievous. "Do you really think Ann has a trapeze in the bedroom?"

"I do," he said. "And maybe a cage. Whips, sheaths, extensions, etc. Their safe word is 'rutabaga.' I think she has some depraved fantasies running through her head. The husband is even worse. At least, it makes me feel better to believe so."

She could picture him sizing up clients as they walked in, noting the bad skin, the sweaty foreheads, the pants pulled up too high, exposing brown socks. She wondered how many of her readers were in sweat pants drinking wine from a coffee cup late at night.

"Do someone else," she said. The waitress came past again, still ignoring them. The woman nodded her chin in the direction of the waitresses' back. Her hair was buzzed close enough to see her skull. One arm was sheathed in tattoos.

"Do her," the woman said.

"There," the man said, "is a person who has decided to work in this coffee shop the rest of her life. Arm-sleeve tattoos proclaim, very loudly, 'I have little to no upward mobility.' She'll work here or somewhere like here and tell herself she enjoys being a waitress. Only she doesn't call herself a waitress. She calls herself a 'barista.' She sings back-up in a band named Muffin Spunk. She sleeps exclusively with women but claims she is bi because bi sounds more hip than gay—like she is all-inclusive, welcoming to anyone—man, woman, whatever. She cut her hair short because her dreads had begun to produce small animals at random intervals. She lives in a studio above a comic book store with an 'adult' section in the back that she has to walk through when she comes home at night, and men in black socks and sandals peeking from beneath trench coats make gurgling noises when she passes through. Showers twice a week. Eats only whole-wheat toast and carrot sticks and spends the day sitting in the window of her apartment with a book in her lap watching business men walk on the street below her."

Her half-smile widened the longer he talked, until she was laughing by the end, snorting a bit. He liked the way she snorted. He decided he liked the way her face was a little pale, as if the reflected screen of her computer late at night had etched itself onto her. He saw her hammering away at her blog, her lips moving slightly as she typed, worrying over commas and semi-colons.

"Now you," he said.

She looked around the coffee shop and nodded. "Over your right shoulder. The guy reading. Don't be obvious."

He fake-stretched and looked. "I couldn't see the title of the book," he said.

They leaned closer together. "It's either *The Seven Habits of Highly Effective People* or something by Ann Coulter. I'm guessing Ann Coulter because of the Republican haircut and the Romney/Ryan button. Keeps entire hairspray companies in business by himself. Grad student in international business, but is really just waiting to take over his father's Fortune 500 company. First name Porter or Miller or Carter, a name he doesn't realize used to be a job someone like him would never have to do. Lives in the pool house of his father's mansion. Tells friends he lives 'on his own.' Trust fund worth eighteen million and some change. Didn't make the soccer team in tenth grade until Daddy donated enough for the school to buy a new bus. Has a girlfriend named Terrin. Aspiring model. Her father owns a chain of outlet stores. She does the commercials. All of them. They change her hair color in each one, give her a mole, dimples, a fake tan. They both somehow manage to look disinterested even when having sex, which isn't often, because they both find it embarrassing. Not being naked or being lustful, but being naked and lustful together. He mostly masturbates to catalogs—doesn't want an electronic trail on his laptop because he might enter politics someday—and she uses her fingers in the shower then feels guilty about her orgasm."

He was laughing loudly, head thrown back, mouth open, and people were turning to look—again—but she didn't care. This was the most fun she'd had in a long time. He slapped the table lightly with his palm as he laughed, but it wasn't pretend, like she imagined him doing with clients, slapping the varnished pine top of his desk at some slightly inappropriate joke one of his clients told. But with his clients his face would be carefully controlled, tie straight, teeth like smooth pills barely visible through salmon-colored lips. The spoons in the coffee cups rattled—the buzz-headed waitress, the barista—still had not re-filled their coffee, and the woman realized she was waiting. Had been waiting a long time for something like this.

"Your turn," she said.

His eyes were filled with light. He rubbed his hands together like a bank thief in an old silent film.

"Now this bitch here," he said, leaning forward and pointing with his chin. "Jesus, will you look at her."

Shannon Burns

LOVE OF NUDE

Some may remember my young period of nude
My long attraction to beige, pink, peach, and of course nude
The nude dress I wore on our trip to the Mojave
The desert, too, being nude
The beauty of the place
The romantic mood I was in
My barely perceptible movements
The nude stone on the path
How it relaxed me
How it became a magic wand to me
The nude you heard in my voice
The nude I saw in others
The nude chiffon
The stirrings
The disappearance into nude
The aloneness with nude
How nude unfurled its chill
How nude changed

Douglas Watson

PINK SLIP

Dear Employee:
   Thank you for your quarter-century of devoted service. You are no longer needed. Goodbye.
   But no, ha ha, of course we jest. That is not how these things are done.
   Dear Employee: When in the course of human events—
Ho ho, that is not the way either. Let's see. Dear Employee: Difficult period, unfortunate necessity, hurts us more than... To right-size or to capsize, that is the question. High waves these days, economic waves, the boat of our once proud industry meets the rogue wave of the future, etc. No life rafts available, sorry, we outsourced the whole life-raft thing last year, no doubt a life raft will appear at any moment on the eastern horizon, from which hope, or at least light, springs eternal, but if not, just call this number, it's, uh... let's see, the number is...
   Dear Employee: Give my love to Barbara? Jim? and your beautiful son/daughter/cat/whatever, we have internships, you know, inside track, don't hesitate. No pay at the outset, but it's a foot in the door, or a paw, children are the future, they grow up so fast, but not cats, cats pretty much stay the same. I don't like cats, never have. The dead eye of a killer, that's what I see when a cat looks at me. If this company were run by cats, whoo-ee, then you'd be in a fix right now, Employee. You would be toyed with. Batted about. Gripped in sharp teeth, shaken, set down, ignored, then you dart your eyes—now? now?—and you make a run for it, and WHAM! the cat has you again. Man, that hurt. It's life or death for you, most likely the latter, but for the cat it is just a game.
   Cats make me sick, Employee.
   Dear Employee: Do not pass Go, do not (although wouldn't that be something?) collect $200, do not even put your things in a box, there are no boxes anymore due to high waves of necessity. You don't really need your things anyway. It doesn't pay to be too materialistic, especially at your age, your thoughts should be turning toward ultimate matters, the life that beats inside you like a heart, etc., etc. The stripping down to what is truly essential: let it now begin. Oh Employee, what I would give

to have the kind of time you're about to have to contemplate what is truly essential! But some of us must work and work, it is our fate. I do not begrudge you your good fortune, Employee.

Dear Employee, how is little Gretchen? Have the doctors made any headway? Or am I mixing up whose daughter…? Ah, well, it'll be easier to keep track of who's who around here from now on, won't it? There's a number to call about insurance, if Gretchen's yours. Or if she isn't! Everyone needs insurance, even people like you who don't have a job, or at any rate that seems to be the spirit of the day. Take, take, take. Ha ha. Let's see, the number is, uh…

Don't cry, Employee. The door is over there, you know what to do. First day of the rest of your life, Employee. Also the last day of your twenty-five years of devoted service, for which we can never, and won't, thank you enough. Today is one of those hinge days, or pivot days, I forget what the poet calls them. The day that is different. One of these days is not like the others—can you spot it? Why, it's today, Employee. Former Employee.

Dear Former Employee: *Why are you still here?*

SAMUEL TOLZMANN   FIGURE UNDER A SHEET

Laura Goldstein

from **LOADED ARC**

birds that fly higher burn out quicker

butterflies battered by traffic act frantic

big name grocers pirate lunchmeat from livestock

collect the eggs and arrange them on hay

seagulls and churchbells adjust the radio

ranging fuzzy phrases move

around the room, the calendar's far flung

meandering clarinet narrative

this is not a judgment call, just trying to reach

a conclusion at the end of the line

you're on. the shore turning over into static

i'm having a hard time hearing, please dial 9

Debbie Hu

i could bolt could i

it's NO afterwards that all the fluster betweenwards
were house, were shy
were what i couldn't, so
not established? so trying
four cups of icicle soup
lollipoply, indifferent
don't doesn't shan't
making a gee irritation swell and a small
row of
hopes in a small voicelies
i hope this poem doesn't get lost too in the oncoming
s - s - s - sw
elter and s - s - s - shhelter me in a second vocabulary
please she swoons in a want of occasion
four spoons in their mouth
carapace and doing and open for occupation

Ruvanee Pietersz Vilhauer

THE RAT TREE

When I decided to take the job, my friend Monica tried to dissuade me.

"You know what that intern who worked there said. It's like another world. If you're trying to prove something, you're going too far," she said.

I saw Mr. Ratnapola for the first time two weeks after I began working at the jail. He was shuffling down the hall of the Rehab Ward towards me, his hands clasped together below his handcuffed wrists. He was a small man. His hair was gray and wispy, a little long in the back. I was surprised to see an inmate who was clearly from South Asia. I had not seen any others. It did not occur to me then that he might be from Sri Lanka too.

When he paused at the door, waiting for his guard to sign him out, he looked up and saw me standing there. Not much of me was visible because I had wrapped my black scarf around my head and neck, and hidden the rest of my body in my boots, gloves and long navy coat. But even then I saw the look of recognition that crossed his face. He did not smile though, or say anything. Instead, he walked past me into the cold wind, through the door the guard opened.

The encounter made me feel calmer than usual. Other days, by the time I walked the path through the jail compound to the door of the Rehab Ward, my heart was thumping and my hands were shaking. It was the walk that made my pounding on the locked Rehab door so desperate, and my voice so thin and high when I identified myself to the guard inside.

My dread about the walk had begun on my first day at the jail. That day, I hadn't been alone, but with the senior psychiatrist, Dr. Denton, who had hired me. He met me at the front gate and made sure that I had left my cell phone at home, as jail regulations required. He introduced me to the three guards who operated the locked gates and the metal detector. They were solid looking, maybe because of the batons, pistols and other hardware that jutted conspicuously from the belts of their blue uniforms. They seemed to know Dr. Denton well. Dr. Denton appeared to be at home in the jail, despite his crisply ironed shirt and his immaculate leather blazer, which made me feel relieved. I had worn jeans and a short tweed jacket, although it seemed odd to go to work dressed so casually. During my interview, Dr. Denton had mentioned that the staff usually wore jeans. My jeans and jacket were new, because I couldn't bear to wear the battered clothes I wore around the house or to the grocery store to my job, even as an entry-level psychiatrist.

Dr. Denton led me out of the guard station into the jail compound, and pointed out the Medical Ward, the kitchens, Women's Blocks A and B, the gym and basketball courts, Men's Blocks C, D, E and F, and in the distance, the Rehab Ward. All the buildings looked the same: gray, boxy and windowless. Dr. Denton walked me down a broad concrete path that lay between the buildings. The sun was out and a pleasant breeze was blowing. This was not going to be so bad, I thought.

"This is the way most of us get to Rehab," he said. "But a few of the younger ladies, the ones who are newcomers, prefer the long way. You turn left here," he said, pointing to a road that branched off past the medical building. "And then you keep going straight to Rehab. If walking under the rat tree doesn't bother you, you might prefer to walk that way."

He said it casually, as if everyone knew what the rat tree was. I wondered whether it was a type of tree commonly found in the U.S., one I had not come across in my ten years here. I pictured a gardener pointing out tree species. Oak. Maple. Apple. Rat. Or maybe it was wrat, or ratte.

I decided to ask Dr. Denton, even if that might emphasize my novice status. "The rat tree?"

"Ah, yes. You can see the top of it from here," he said, pointing. There was a treetop visible in the distance, looming above the drab roof of the kitchen building. It must have been the only tree in the jail compound. It was some sort of spruce, and the top of it was thick with leaves.

"It's nice that there's such a big tree in here," I said. "It makes the compound seem more pleasant somehow."

Dr. Denton looked at me, his head tilted slightly. "That tree is full of rats," he said. "That's where all the rats from the kitchens go. They take shelter there. It's warmer in there than on the ground. There are no holes for them in these concrete walls."

"But rats don't climb trees!" I said. "At least, I've never heard of that."

"These do," Dr. Denton said, not argumentatively, but simply stating a fact. "They've jumped down onto people walking under that tree. Once, several jumped down onto Therese, our filing assistant. And Anne Chen, she's one of the nurses in Medical."

"Jumped onto them?"

"Jumped, fell, I don't know. They said jumped," Dr. Denton said, shrugging. "You aren't fond of rats, I gather."

"Not really, no," I said, wanting to seem professional. It was not easy, because the thought of the rat tree had made my throat close up.

I couldn't even bear rats when they were dead and barely recognizable, preserved in formaldehyde. I had tried to dissect one once, during a group project in a pre-med biology class. But the rat lying there in front of me, gray and leathery, had filled me with such revulsion that I couldn't cut into it. Each time I touched it with my scalpel, my hand jerked back involuntarily. The others in the group had stared at me, astonished and amused. I was embarrassed that my behavior was so irrational. Eventually, someone else had done the dissection, while I stood in the background, trying not to gag. I had been careful not to register for any more classes that required interacting with rats, alive or dead. It was difficult enough to suppress my disgust when I saw photographs of them in textbooks, their skin peeled back to display their slimy-looking insides.

"Well, then you can just take this other route. It's shorter anyway," Dr. Denton said. We walked on past the front of the kitchens and the women's blocks, towards the gym. Outside the gym, there was a basketball court enclosed by a high fence topped with coils of barbed wire. A group of male inmates in orange uniforms was playing basketball. About twenty or thirty other inmates were lounging around or seated on steel benches at the edge of the court.

As we came up to the fence, one of the inmates whistled. The sound stood out clearly against the diffuse noise of voices and laughter. Another inmate yelled, "Yo, baby! Where *you* from?" Others began turning around and whistling or calling out, and soon, a group of inmates had gathered along the perimeter of the fence. One of them, a tall, muscular man with a boxer's nose and a completely shaved head, looked me directly in the eye, cupped both his hands over his crotch, ground his hips, and said, "Take your clothes off for me, baby."

Before I could get over the shock I felt at this utterance, another man yelled, "Yeah, let's see what's under them clothes, huh?" Yet another man, whose smooth skin and baby-faced features made him seem much too young to be in jail, pressed his body against the wire of the fence, and crooned, "Wrap that hair around me, honey! Wrap it around me, oh yeah, oh honey!" There were humming cries of, "Mmm-mmh!" Some of the men stuck their lips to the fence and made slurping, kissing noises. Others laughed.

I looked straight ahead, at the road, and tried to seem unconcerned. My ears and face felt hot, and it was difficult to fight the urge to run. Behind me, I heard a voice shout out, "Ooooh, that ass! I want some of that!"

Dr. Denton turned around and said, "Cut it out, you guys."

To me, he said, "Don't let it get to you. Ignore them. They'll be more respectful once they get to know who you are."

I heard one of the guards inside the fence say, "Back, back! Get back from that fence!" But there was not much enthusiasm in his voice, and the inmates did not respond to his order. The whistles and catcalls followed us until we were out of earshot.

My dreams that night were filled with men in orange suits chasing me around shadowy buildings, and heavy, hairless rats that leaped down onto me from fences, their writhing tails burrowing greedily under my clothes.

I had held other clinical positions before, during my training. They'd been at outpatient clinics in upscale Philadelphia suburbs. My patients had worn understated clothes and shoes polished to a high sheen. They had expected the best. Only one of my patients had questioned my credentials and asked to see a more experienced clinician. She was a stern middle-aged professor, a scholar of ancient Roman history. Her primary care physician had referred her to my clinic because of her constant concern over the possibility that she might accidentally swallow her tongue while lecturing to her students. I had not wanted to suggest that her worries were excessive. Most of my other patients had been eager to assume that I would not have been hired unless I was highly competent. Their confidence had rubbed off on me, and I had been relatively comfortable diagnosing problems and prescribing medication and psychotherapy.

At least, that was what I had thought until I asked my primary supervisor, Dr. Lockwood, for a recommendation. It was not that he wrote a poor reference. But he ended his careful evaluation with these words: *Although mild-mannered and not one to take risks, Dr. Peiris is an astute clinician, and will do fine in a safe and nurturing setting.*

I sorted the walk-in closet in my apartment into two sections. In one section, I hung all the clothes that I could wear to the jail, and in the other section, the clothes I could not. The clothes I could wear to the jail were the ones that could cover and conceal: thick, long-sleeved shirts that buttoned high, baggy sweaters, long jackets and cardigans that fell over my hips, loose pants and ankle-length skirts.

The cold wind that blew through the jail compound allowed me to wear an additional layer outdoors, usually my long navy overcoat. I started pinning up my hair so that it would be less visible too. But even with all that, I worried. Each day, when I came to the fork between the short road and the long one, I hesitated, trying to force myself to choose the road that led under the rat tree. I never could. The thought of the rats kept me on the path that ran past the basketball courts. I kept my eyes down, and tried to keep my mind occupied by thinking about positions to which I could apply when the next job season arrived.

My fantasies did not sustain me, though. By the time I arrived at the door of the Rehab Ward, I felt completely exposed, my clothing stripped from me by the inmates' shouts.

I wished I had listened to my parents. "You can give up your apartment and come back home for a long vacation until you find a good job," my mother had said when I called about my new position.

"Ma, this is a good job. It will give me great experience," I said.

"You'll be fraternizing with the scum of society, Preethi," my father said. I could hear him tapping his pencil on his desk, the way he did when he was irritated.

"Fraternizing? I'll be seeing patients who need help," I said. "This is not Sri Lanka. The jails are decent places." At the time, I had never set foot in a jail in the United States, let alone in Sri Lanka. My interview with Dr. Denton had happened at a local hotel, during the American Psychiatric Association's annual convention.

I was uncomfortable when inmates were with me in the so-called consulting room, which was a small, bare-walled, windowless cube lit by two fluorescent bulbs. The regulation furniture was all plastic, designed so that no pieces of chairs or tables could be secretly removed and used as weapons or means for suicide.

Dr. Denton and Dr. Holmes, the other senior psychiatrist, saw the men who lived in dorms within the Rehab Ward, men who suffered from severe depression or who were in the early stages of recovery from drug addiction. Most of my patients were men who lived in other blocks of the jail. Each day, guards brought them to me for brief consultations. They came in groups of five or ten. They lounged on chairs in the starkly lit corridor, a few feet away from the open door of the consulting room, waiting their turn.

I sat by the door. It had a Plexiglas pane in it, so the guard who strolled along the corridor outside could see that I was not in trouble, even if I closed it. I left the door open. The inmates came in one at a time. I did not engage them in much conversation. I asked them what the problem was, keeping my eyes down as much as possible, looked in their file and prescribed medication, mostly anti-anxiety drugs or anti-depressants.

One of my first patients was Phil Simmons. He was the man with the boxer's nose and the shaved head that I had seen on the basketball court on my first day. Dr. Denton had already told me about his history. He was one of the regulars in the jail. This was his fifth incarceration, although he was only forty.

"He's the one to watch out for," Dr. Denton said.

"Why is he here?" I asked.

"Robbery, this time," Dr. Denton said. "I think he likes it better in here than out on the streets. Some of these men have an easier time in here than in the world. They have a safe place to sleep, plenty of heat, three meals a day."

He saw me grimace. "You don't like bologna, I see," he said, smiling. He handed me a small sheaf of papers. "Some things for you to look through," he said. "I don't know how familiar you are with malingering. There's a lot of that here. Save the meds for the men who need it."

I had never come across a case of malingering during my training. "You don't have to worry about that," I said. "You won't find me giving out medications to people who are faking."

Dr. Denton smiled again. "Good to have a capable clinician onboard," he said.

Mr. Simmons looked even larger in the consulting room than he had out on the basketball court. The plastic chair across from me looked absurdly small in comparison to him. He did not look like he belonged in the room. The sight of him sitting there reminded me of an illustration I had seen in a book when I was a child: a circus tiger balanced on a tiny stool, baring its teeth at a costumed tamer.

"How can I help you, Mr. Simmons?" I said, surreptitiously wiping the sweat off my palms onto my jeans. I wished I had not forgotten to get my white doctor's coat from the closet in the file room, where I had hung it up when I arrived that morning.

Mr. Simmons leaned back in his chair and grinned. His front teeth were stained brownish yellow, and the upper middle two were chipped. Reddish blonde stubble marked his ruddy cheeks, and a tattoo of a bleeding rose covered his forearm. He stretched out his legs. His hands were resting on his crotch. "I can think of a buncha ways," he said.

I wondered if he could see how hard my heart was thumping. I tried to breathe deeply. "I see you were on Valium the last time you were in jail," I said, looking at his file, and avoiding looking at him. "For anxiety?"

"Yeeees," said Mr. Simmons, his tone mocking. "Thing is, I'm so tense I just can't get me to sleep. Keep having this dream and it wakes me up. This broad comes to see me. Takes off her clothes. Every fucking stitch. I'm staring at her bare ass and her tits. They're big, y'know, juicy. I'm just getting ready to get into it with her. Then she walks off. Ass swinging like nothing you ever seen. There's this big old knife in my hand. I run with it, huh? Almost get to her. Then I wake up. Every time."

I looked up from the file. He was still grinning, picking at his teeth with his overgrown thumbnail.

"Bet you never had a dream like that."

"I can't say I have," I said, turning my eyes back to the file, wishing I sounded less apprehensive.

"Good soft bed you sleep in, I bet," he said. I could hear the smirk in his voice. "All covered up. Butt naked under those covers, huh?" His chair grated across the floor.

I drew another deep breath, nausea rising in my stomach. I did not respond.

He was quiet for a minute then. "No. Not your type o' dreams," he said. "Not the type to be knifing anyone. What d'you dream about then? Books?" He laughed.

"I'll renew your prescription," I said. All I wanted was for him to get out of the room.

"And I'll see you next week," said Mr. Simmons. "I'll be waiting." He pulled himself out of his chair.

After he left, I went down the corridor and into the small staff kitchenette adjacent to the filing room. I locked the door and looked at myself in the mirror. I looked too young to be doing this job.

I thought about what my ex-fiancé had said in the note he had sent me from Colombia. In addition to informing me that he had chosen to continue his Médecins Sans Frontières position, he had denounced my inability to commit two years to working in a country he said was safe enough, but which I knew had one of the highest rates of drug violence in the world. You can go on living your sheltered life if you want, he had said, but that's not how I want to live.

I wet a paper towel and wiped my face. Then I went back to the consulting room. My experiences with the rest of my patients that day did nothing to increase my confidence.

Monica called the following day, which was a Saturday, thankfully free of the jail. I was lying in bed, feeling anxious and trying to read an article about malingering. "Well, do you like it?" she asked. I could hear a little malice in her voice.

"I love it," I said, which was what I had also told my parents. "It's pretty different from Clarendon, of course. But I feel like I'm really making a difference. And the men are just, you know, people. Like you and me. Just people who happened to take the wrong path."

"I have to hand it to you," Monica said. "Honestly, I didn't think you'd be able to cut it. But you've adjusted so quickly."

"I know," I said. "I'm surprised I've been able to. But listen, I have to go. I was just rushing out the door. I'll call you."

The first time Mr. Ratnapola came into the consulting room, he called me "Mrs. Peiris," even though he knew I was a doctor. His handcuffs were off. He shuffled to the table and sat down.

I said, "I'm not married."

He looked at my bare ring finger, and nodded, looking a little uncomfortable. He did not say anything else about it, but he stopped referring to me in any way at all.

I knew by then that he was from Sri Lanka. I had heard from Dr. Denton. We were the only people from Sri Lanka he knew. Mr. Ratnapola probably knew we were from the same country too, from my name, but he did not say anything about it.

"So, Mr. Ratnapola," I said. "How can I help you?"

"Sleeping," he said. "Can't sleep. Everything else is okay. Food also, I don't mind. The men are okay, they leave me alone. I help people with their cases. Read law books from the library. But can't sleep."

"I can give you some pills," I said. "But you will have to come back once a week. I can only give you a few at a time. And you can't keep taking these for long. It's a short-term solution."

He nodded as he came in the next week. "The pills helped," he said.

"You are sleeping well?"

"Yes," he said. "But you, you are not. Black circles under the eyes. Not a good sign."

"I've been staying up too late," I said.

"Worrying," he said.

I nodded, and opened his file. "I can prescribe the same pills for another week," I said.

The following week, my morning staff meeting ran late. My patients were already outside the consulting room, leaning in a jagged row against the corridor wall, when I came into the Rehab Ward. As usual, my hands were shaking as I pulled off my gloves. The dreaded walk through the compound had been particularly taxing because in my nervousness, I had dropped the files I had been carrying in front of the basketball court. The inmates on the court, led by Phil Simmons, had abandoned their games and lined up at the fence, whistling and cheering while I chased down papers and crouched on the ground, fighting my nausea, to pick them up.

Inside Rehab, I walked past the patients outside the consulting room without looking at them. I nodded to the guard at the door of the room and went in. Mr. Ratnapola was the first patient to come in.

"How are you?" he said.

"Fine, okay," I said. I was still trying to catch my breath and the nausea was still lurking.

"You don't look so fine."

"I was hurrying," I said. "To get here."

"Not only that," he said.

"No." I realized my face was a little sweaty, even though it was cold outside.

"The men are bothering you?" he asked.

"The men? Yes, I suppose so," I said. "I still haven't got used to this place."

"Different from the world," he said.

"I hate walking past the basketball courts," I said.

"Simmons. That fellow is the ring leader," he said.

The guard looked in through the Plexiglas pane, and I realized that I had forgotten to wear my white coat again. Mr. Ratnapola's file was lying closed on the table in front of me. I opened it.

"The sleeping pills are working well?" I asked him.

"Yes, okay," he said. I renewed his prescription for another week.

The next week, I asked Mr. Ratnapola where he was from in Sri Lanka.

Mr. Ratnapola clicked his tongue. "How can I tell you that?" he said, sounding irritated. "Next thing, it'll be all over the Daily News. Harischandra Ratnapola Talks To Jail Worker In States."

This had not occurred to me, but I could see the truth in what he said. Sri Lanka was a small country. Word spread quickly. I leaned over and pushed the door closed. The click of the latch sounded loud.

"Everything you tell me is confidential," I said. "Unless I get a subpoena. I can't talk about my patients with anyone. It's against the law."

Mr. Ratnapola snorted. "What law?" he said. "They're going to enforce American law in Sri Lanka also?"

"I suppose not. But there's also the ethics of it. I don't talk about my patients, here or there."

Mr. Ratnapola was silent for a while. Then he nodded.

"Kandy," he said. "I am from Kandy. My brother is a doctor also. Internal Medicine. He works in Kandy General Hospital. Srinath Ratnapola. Do you know?"

"No," I said. "I did college and medical school here. I only go back in the summers, to see my parents."

"What do your parents do?"

"Thaththi is a lawyer," I said. "Senior State Counsel."

"Willy Peiris?"

"No, Denzil," I said. "Willy is my uncle. Thaththi's brother."

"Your mother? She is also working?"

"She's a dentist. Private practice."

"They are in Colombo?" he asked.

"Yes," I said.

"Ah, right," he said. "My wife's brother-in-law's cousins are all in Colombo. They might know them."

It was strange to be having this ordinary conversation with an inmate in the jail, one who was accused of no less a crime than murder. His file had told me that, and that his bail was a very large sum of money. I knew no details about the allegations against him, but it seemed unlikely that he could be a murderer. I did not want to discuss the topic with him. I had been warned about the legal and ethical hazards of discussing the inmates' alleged crimes.

When Mr. Ratnapola came in the next week, I saw that his hair was freshly cut, very close to his scalp.

"A new haircut," I said.

He ran his hand over the stubble on his head, and smiled. "Makes me feel more at home," he said.

"I don't know if that's a good thing," I said.

"Good to feel at home," he said, leaning back in the plastic chair.

"When do you think you'll get out?" I asked. It was only after I said the words that I realized I was getting into dangerous territory.

Mr. Ratnapola shrugged. "You mean when I will go to prison?"

"No," I said, hastily. I did not want him to think that I believed he was guilty. "I mean, when is your court date?"

"Not for another month," he said. He seemed unconcerned.

"It must be hard. For you, and for your family," I said.

Mr. Ratnapola rubbed his cheeks with his hands. He had let his nails get overgrown. "They are in the world," he said. "My wife is with my daughter. She will look after her mother."

He covered his face with his hands for a moment, and then rubbed his cheeks again. I saw that there were tears in the corners of his eyes. "She is at Yale University now. Law school. This is what she wanted to do. But before she wanted to study women's rights. Now she is doing criminal law."

"You must be proud of her," I said. I could not think of anything I could say to make him feel better.

Mr. Ratnapola nodded. He pressed his thumbs into the corners of his eyes, and then dragged them down his face, leaving wet lines on his cheeks. "Her husband was beating her," he said. "He wanted to know where she was every minute. He forbade her to apply to law school. Even get a job. See her parents."

I was beginning to feel uneasy. "I have to remind you," I said. "I don't talk about my patients. But if I was subpoenaed, I would be legally bound to answer questions in court, even if I didn't think that was the ethical way to treat my patients."

Mr. Ratnapola nodded again. He looked at the Plexiglas pane in the door. The guard was not there. "I am only telling you about my family," he said. "Nothing that you want to write notes about. You won't even remember any of this."

He did not wait for me to reply. I put down my pen. "He was a tourist," he said. "Can you believe? We were on holiday. In Galle. Coromandel Hotel. My cousin is the assistant manager. Eric was sitting at the next table. Having rice and curry. Even eating dried fish. Just like a local fellow. That's how we met. Got to be very friendly. We invited him to come home. Tilaka liked him. My wife. Nice fellow. Those days, he was nice. Nice-looking also. Skin was red like a boiled prawn, but nice face. Good smile. He started writing to Sumathi after he went off, back to the States."

"Sumathi is your daughter?" I wanted to hear his story, although I knew the inmates waiting outside would be getting restless.

"My only," Mr. Ratnapola said. "Tilaka had four miscarriages after that."

"I'm sorry to hear that," I said.

"What for sorry?" Mr. Ratnapola said. "Our karma. Sumathi is enough. Very good girl. Bright also. But she got fooled by Eric. We also got fooled. But can't say. Maybe he changed. Eight years ago, that was. Person can change."

"Yes," I said.

"Eric was the one who said we should come here. He was earning enough to sponsor us. Stockbroker. Good job. After we got citizenship, he helped to start the business. Shop, we have. Had. Now, of course, sold. Convenience store."

"It sounds like he was a pretty nice guy," I said.

Mr. Ratnapola hunched his shoulders. He put his head in his hands. He did not look up when he spoke. "Before, yes. But then all this jealousy. Always shouting at Sumathi. Twice she came with broken hands. We took her to the hospital. Bruises all the time."

"Why didn't she leave?" I asked.

"Not so easy. He said he would kill her. Find her and kill her. And us also. Who knows if he was telling the truth? Also, she was attracted to him. Even with all this. Sometimes everything was fine and dandy."

"It would have been more rational to leave," I said.

Mr. Ratnapola made a snorting sound. "Rational? We are all making irrational choices, no. But after we make the choice, then have to stick to it. Embrace it. That is what I always told Sumathi. When she was small. And she was trying to embrace her choice. Stay in the marriage."

"So what happened?"

"He died," said Mr. Ratnapola. "Hit on the head. Blood everywhere." He rubbed his eyes and then folded his arms across his chest. "But now Sumathi is free."

I nodded, not sure what I could say.

"It is hard to see what young women go through," he said. "You also. Something has to be done."

"I could leave if I am not happy here," I said. "But leaving in the middle of the year seems like a defeat."

He was silent for a while. "I have friends," he said finally. "They can send a message. Not hurt Simmons too much, you understand. Only get him to stop. But weapons, they don't have." I was not sure I understood what he meant.

He picked up the plastic coffee cup I had brought from the Rehab kitchenette. "A piece of glass would be enough. Small, so that no one would see." He slid the cup over to me. "Think about it." There was no expression on his face.

The realization of what he meant made me recoil from the table. "Are you telling me ...?"

He glanced at the shut door. "I am not saying anything," he said. "But you have to play with the rules in the place. And this is not the same world as outside." He pushed back his chair. "Think is all I am saying."

I did not tell Monica, my parents or anyone else about Mr. Ratnapola's suggestion. Over the following week, I tried, from time to time, to think about what he had said. But my mind slid around his words. At first they seemed simply ridiculous, and then too unpleasant to contemplate.

I had no intention of taking any contraband to work on Tuesday.

Maybe it was frustration with my daily nausea that made me drop my nearly empty coffee cup shortly before I left my apartment. When I crouched over the ceramic fragments scattered across the kitchen tiles, I remembered how the inmates had called out and rattled the basketball court fence as I picked up my fallen papers, and the look I had seen on Mr. Simmons's face when I finally got to my feet. Before dumping the cup fragments into the trash can, I picked out one piece and laid it on my palm. It was a little smaller than my thumb and not particularly sharp. It looked like a tooth, I thought: long, brown-stained and slightly curved, like a large rat's incisor. On impulse, I put it in my bag, tucked under my folded doctor's coat.

The guards at the gate knew me by then. I walked through into the jail compound without any trouble.

I kept my head down and hurried past the basketball court, trying to ignore the catcalls and the sight of Phil Simmons standing at the fence, massaging his crotch.

My doctor's coat, when I took it out of my bag, was stained with coffee from the cup shard I had pushed under it. I was dabbing at the stain with a tissue when Mr. Ratnapola shuffled into the consulting room.

"That will come out," he said. "No one will notice."

I nodded, feeling more anxious than I usually did in his presence. I pulled his file out of the stack on the table.

"That is not why I came today," he said. "Only to see if I can help. You have thought about what I said?"

I got up from my chair and shut the door.

"I can't talk about that," I said, but I could not help looking over at my bag, where the piece of ceramic lay hidden.

"There is no need to talk," he said. I saw that he had noticed my bag; I usually left it in the file room.

"I could leave," I said. "Or put up with it. It gets better, Dr. Denton says."

Mr. Ratnapola opened his hands in a small gesture. "That choice, you have to make," he said.

He watched me quietly while thoughts flooded my mind, about what crime I would be committing, about the Hippocratic oath I had taken, about how many people might get injured even with one ceramic tooth, and about what my parents might say. Then I remembered the reference Dr. Lockwood had written. Was this another instance of not being willing to take a risk? Was I so afraid to play by the new rules in this place that I would rather give up and leave?

I glanced at the Plexiglas pane in the door. The guard was nowhere to be seen. My bag was lying on the floor by my chair. It would be easy to take the piece of ceramic out and pass it to Mr. Ratnapola across the table, I thought. Or maybe I could drop it on the floor. It would barely make a sound. Dropping it could almost be accidental. He would pick it up and roll it into the waistband of his pants, perhaps, or tuck it into the hem of his uniform shirt.

I do not know how long I sat there with my thoughts and Mr. Ratnapola silent across from me.

Later, I thought there had been a fifty-fifty chance of deciding one way or the other. It did not seem implausible that I might have chosen to slip Mr. Ratnapola a light sliver of ceramic in those circumstances and in that world, even if that meant committing a crime that could have ended in someone's death or serious injury.

But I did not do it. I bent and shut the flap of my bag. "All I can hope is that it gets better soon," I said.

Mr. Ratnapola did not speak for a while. Then he said, surprisingly, "You are tough." He rose abruptly from his seat. "No pills today. I am going to try without." He went out of the room without looking at me again.

When Mr. Simmons came in, a half hour later, I was swallowing the last of the coffee in my plastic cup.

He sat across from me, and leaned back, his thighs spread wide. "Spilt something right there," he said, grinning, his eyes fixed on the stained breast pocket of my white coat.

"How can I help you, Mr. Simmons?" I said, trying to ignore my discomfort.

"Just sittin' here is helping me no end," he said, covering his crotch with his thick fingers. "Y'know what I'm saying. And that Valium, that's the cream on the cake." There was a wet sound as he sucked air through his front teeth.

Maybe it was Mr. Ratnapola's offer of help, or the knowledge that the ceramic chip was lying in the bag next to me, or the fact that I had brought the chip to the jail, or simply the choice I had just made, that allowed me to look Mr. Simmons in the eye for the first time. "What problem do you have, Mr. Simmons, that makes you need the Valium?" I said.

A crease appeared in his forehead, and then he showed his teeth in a sneer. "Well, now. Haven't I told you about them dreams that keep waking me up? This one broad, y'see, with an ass like a ripe ..."

"Yes, I remember you told me several times about your dreams, Mr. Simmons," I said, forcing myself to keep my gaze steady on his face. "Is that the main problem?"

He dragged a nail across his front tooth. "Hmmm-uhhh. If I can't sleep, how can I get me some of that ..."

I interrupted him again. "Well, I am sorry to hear that, but I can't prescribe any more Valium." I saw his mouth drop open a little as I slapped his file shut.

He planted his hands, bunched into fists, on the table between us and leaned his bulk towards me. "See here ..."

I stood up as casually as I could. "I think you will get used to sleeping without the pills," I said.

Then I called out to the guard and informed him that Mr. Simmons had completed his visit.

It was only when Mr. Simmons was leaving the room that I noticed the resigned slump of his shoulders. It occurred to me that I had not seen him from any angle but head on. The years had not been kind to him, I saw; at forty, he was already bowed with the weight of them.

"Let me know how you fare," I said.

He left without glancing back.

Three weeks passed. The weather was getting warmer. I could no longer wear my long coat to work. I thought about wearing one of my baggy long-sleeved shirts, untucked over my jeans. Instead, though, I wore a light fitted tee shirt, tucked in. I left my hair unconcealed, tied up in a ponytail. Instead of carrying my white doctor's coat to work in my bag, folded up, as I had in the past, I put it on over my clothes. Although the coffee stain had not washed out completely, it was only faintly visible.

There were puddles in the jail compound from the rain the night before. I wondered whether to take the road past the rat tree. I had walked that way a few times by then. Initially, it had not been by choice, but because a construction crew jackhammering down to the plumbing system had closed off the path past the basketball court. I had clenched my jaw and given the tree a wide berth, alert to the risk of rats falling from the branches above. But nothing had happened, and since then, I had ventured that way a few more times. There had been no ill effects, perhaps because the rats were as watchful of me as I was of them.

But on this day, I chose the shorter path. The wind was gusting as I walked towards the basketball court. As I drew closer, I heard someone say, "Hello, Doc." It was Mr. Ratnapola. He was sitting on the bench by the side of the court. I had not seen him there before. It was hard to distinguish him from the others milling around, all in their orange uniforms.

I stopped and walked over to the fence. The men by the fence became silent. I could feel their eyes on me. "Hello, Mr. Ratnapola," I said. "How are you? Is everything going well?"

"Yes," he said. "Fine, everything is okay, Doc."

"Good to hear," I said.

I caught sight of Mr. Simmons some distance away.

"Mr. Simmons," I said. "How's it going?"

"Survivin', Doc," Mr. Simmons said, his tone grudging. "More or less."

Rain began to fall as I turned away, flecking my stained white coat and the orange uniforms of the men waiting by the fence.

I nodded to the men and walked the short distance to my consulting room, listening to the thud of the basketballs as they went back to their games.

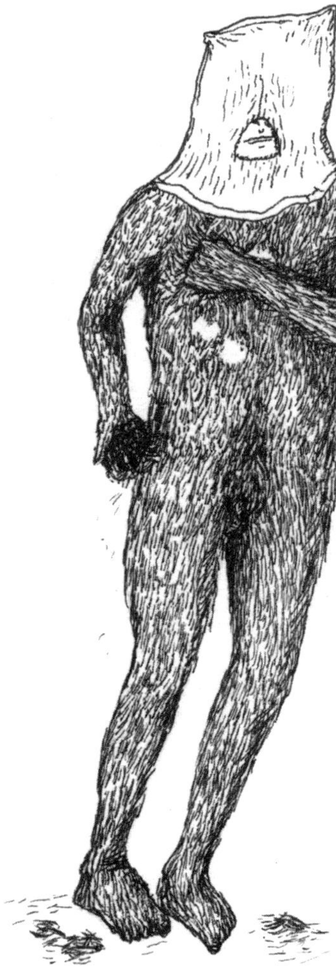

Steve Rogggenbook

FROM I LOVE MUSIC

memories of crying while eating pancakes

painting in jessicas kitchen

eating chocolate covered pretzels made by jessicas mom and
    playing tony hawk 4

memories of listening to rap while driving a tractor

going to small nearby towns such as minden city when i was first
    getting to know jessica

riding in my best friends car in high school

kissing my girlfriend and taking off my shirt and throwing it onto
    her friends head who was sitting in the room

memories of listening to hopesfall and crying after breaking up
    with my girl friend

how do we live stephen

why does it hurt

why do i miss every thing

Natasha Lvovich

SANDY CHRONICLES

Coney Island, Brooklyn

Titanic

My windows are taped in crosses like in Soviet war movies. The wind is bombing in gusts, and trees are bending to the ground. High tide and full moon, they say: the Grand Ball at Satan's. The TV and the lights in the house suddenly make a dry *ssch-pooh* and the power is out. Here we are. I light the candles and glance out the window at the parking lot downstairs.

The water has come in so quickly that within minutes the parking lot is a sea, the extension of the ocean filling the beach, the boardwalk, the street, and now spreading further inland, in and around buildings with dark unseeing windows. I can hear it from my fourth floor island splashing nonchalantly against my building façade, as if it had been there all along. I am perched above the infinite ocean.

All of a sudden, the dark silence explodes with a bright lightening and a loud cacophony of car alarms in crying voices: some wailing, some yelping, and some demanding. I think I hear my own little car crying but then I remember it has no alarm. Scriabin's *Prometheus* in sinister hues and notes of white and orange lasts for a few minutes until the cars sink one by one and begin floating, bumping into each other and into the building slowly, soundlessly, almost gracefully. Dark silence, without reflections and movement, arrives. Titanic has sunk.

Hurricane Intimacy

I suddenly don't care about the consequences. Nothing rational matters: four years incommunicado, the deleted number, the whited-out name ... I am alone in the dark, surrounded by black water, facing a long night. I am helpless as a child, and I am allowed.

The civilization we have known has suddenly vanished—except for my cell phone. I cannot call but can still text, standing in one particular spot in the kitchen, persistently pressing the 'send' button until the words, my little messenger birds, finally take off and fly away.

He is here, holding me and whispering in my ear: I've been worried about you. I miss you. Do you need anything? I can drive right in. My car is submersible ...

Oh no, he has no idea what it is like here, but I courageously say, I am OK, thank you. I have a bathtub filled with water, a few candles, and a flashlight. You are as sweet as ever. It is pretty apocalyptic here. Water is all around. It keeps coming.

He is whispering: Are you in the evacuation zone, Love? Why didn't you leave? Where is Julia? How is Baba?

The most intimate words ever—timelessness, tenderness, connection. They are gliding, like a gulp of vodka, down my throat into the chest and staying there warmly and whitely. I am not alone.

He keeps whispering on my tiny screen: It is frightening now, but tomorrow will be better. The water will recede. Try to relax now, eat and have a glass of wine.

It will never recede. How can so much water recede? I've just taken a sleeping pill and will try to go to sleep. Will turn off my phone now to save the battery. Thank you.

I go to bed and hug my pillow in a brisk wing-like movement, as if swimming freestyle, with my mouth reaching out for air, my head sideways on the water, the pillow, the water, the pillow. I am sliding gracefully and freely. My body is strong and healthy. My thoughts are sweet, like those on a night before a date. I drift on.

When I wake up, grey light seeps from the window. The water has receded, just as he promised. Uprooted trees and muddy cars with steamed windows are on sidewalks, on lawns, in the middle of the road, or smashed into a collapsed wavy fence. The parking lot is a cemetery of cars.

A text on my phone, last night's whisper: Good night Love. I will be thinking of you. Tomorrow will check on you. I always want to check on you.

I love this English tense—present indefinite ... Come and check on me! Check on me! But the storm is over. And my phone makes the dying-swan-dance final movement.

> *What birds plunge through is not the intimate space*
> *in which you see all forms intensified.*[1]

---

[1] Rilke, Rainer Maria, ["What birds plunge through is not the intimate space"], *The Selected Poetry of Rainer Maria Rilke*. Trans. and Ed. Stephen Mitchell. New York: Random House, 1982

The Day of All Saints

Post-Sandy Ocean Parkway at Brighton Beach *is* the beach, only muddy, with mounds of sand and garbage. As in an outlandish post-nuclear TV series, dead cars are frozen in their final moment: some are burned skeletons, some are incongruously stuck in the middle of the avenue at an oblique angle, some solitary, their rears sitting on benches, some coupled, and some in ménage à trois collisions, with their windows opened or taped with black plastic bags. Inside, sand and water.

Disasters look exactly like movies—a monstrous fantasy converging with reality, minus popcorn, with the audience transported onto the screen somehow.

Zombie passers-by are staring down, their tired eyes zeroing in on the pavement, their clothes as if bleached and colorless, their boots and pants covered by red mud. Many are carrying big plastic bags filled with Greek yogurts and juices already on sale at flooded powerless stores. Small groups form around these sidewalk vendors, like ants, in complete silence. Cut-off conversations echo in ghostly Russian voices: ... no we have no water ... my charger was in the car ... Con Edison ... yes I called the insurance ... she has Verizon ... there will be no school ... Geico ... National Guard ... FEMA ... Many are squatting to take pictures of "the movie" with their (still charged) phones. For their insurance? For posterity?

The air is moist, warm, almost tropical for November, and a group of young people from *St. Petersburg*, the Russian bookstore, is drying CDs with paper towels, sitting outside on folding chairs and chatting with insouciance. At a corner, a table with wet Russian calendars and a handwritten note: "Take—free." But nobody wants them: time is endless, dateless, unstructured—one big heavy lump of present filled with basic needs and concerns, water, food, light, warmth, family. One day at a time is a motto, so familiar, so Russian from generations of survival, and I suddenly get it, my acquired-in- America love for Protestant structure—it is hope, future, safety, control, predictability.

A Trump Village building on Ocean Parkway has its own electricity generator, and, rumor has it, people are allowed to charge cell phones there. Crowds of Russians mixed with a few native Brooklynites are in the lobby, where connectivity-hungry clusters are squatting around the outlets. At once, I strategically assess the situation with my Soviet-trained eye, zeroing in on a line that seems shorter and multitasking to seize and hold two of them simultaneously. For that, one needs to engage in small talk all the while keeping one's eyes and ears open for arising opportunities.

And indeed, such an opportunity materializes almost at once: a woman ahead of me asks her daughter to take me to her other line, which of course she was also holding, and where her phone would be finished charging momentarily (wink wink). I sit down on a pile of Yellow Pages, ready to jump in, like a tiger, to get hold of the outlet.

Next to me, hooked to the same outlet, a family is shepherding a few phones at a twin extension, their faces absorbed in the task of watching the electricity flow and checking the displays every thirty seconds. I try to engage in small talk, but nobody responds. Nobody smiles. The grandpa complains to his son-in-law that it takes forever to charge a phone in this building and that once charged, the phone's power is immediately spent! I suggest with a smile that there must be poor quality of electricity here—and he confirms with a stern face: indeed, electricity is not good in this building. Echoing this sentiment, another old man, his phone already charging, jumps in to unplug his phone and triumphantly cries out, "I found another, better outlet!" (The Russian word he uses sounds like "aperture").

In another corner, where an outlet looks like a pyramid of extensions and strips, an elderly couple in heavy winter coats is loudly bickering. Sitting on the floor, a woman in a crooked wig is asking every man who enters—never a woman—if he has a knife to open a can, since she is awfully thirsty and got this good orange juice, and how come men don't carry those pocket knives with can openers anymore ... What happened to real men?

I am wondering, too.

At that moment, as if responding to our question, a swift man in his early sixties, business-like and well-shaven, storms in—we are all in awe. He walks straight to our charging station with "poor electricity," takes out four laptops, three phones, a power strip, and a bunch of wires and cables from a duffel bag, nodding toward the group for permission to hook up his equipment. Silent scene. Somebody exhales, "Nastoyashiy muzhchina ...!" (A real man!).

When the thirsty woman in a crooked wig repeats her plea for the juice, the "real man"—oh so predictably!—pulls out a pocket knife and confidently digs a hole in her can. Yes! We are all relieved to see the woman finally quench her thirst. A moment of dreamy erotic silence hangs over this lobby corner ...

About three hours later, when my phone displays "Fully Charged," I slowly crawl home, holding my phone in the air like an antenna, trying to catch a connection: call my mother, who has no light, no heat, no water but amazingly has a working landline phone; call my teenage daughter, who is cut off from me in Manhattan, and text my dear friends—for news, love, hugs. Three of them have lost their homes.

When I walk into the lobby, something feels different. The tiles are still muddy, the air moist. I start climbing the stairs, both reluctant and happy, and suddenly realize that the staircase and hallways are not dark! When I walk into my apartment, the lights in the kitchen and living room greet me, just as I had left them in the long gone pre-Sandy era. *Que la lumière soit!* The water is running, the refrigerator is humming.

Later at night the door bell rings: two kids in Halloween costumes. Trick or Treat! Their mother is waiting in the hallway, acting out normalcy from behind the corner. Halloween ...? I am shocked and relieved at the same time. I am so sorry, I've got no candy.

NPZ (No Power Zone)

On the tenth day after the storm, Coney Island Resort is officially Coney Island Desolation. Mounds of sand fill sidewalks; most street lights are still out; ever-green is now ever-muddy; dust and sand are swirling in the wind. Sea Gate community is destroyed, its homes cracked open; and in the "projects," I hear, extreme powerlessness is both literal and metaphoric. From my balcony, I hear the sirens and see a long convoy of Humvees heading in the direction of the "barrio."

The college is still closed; schools are closed; banks are closed. There is no gas in the city; the subway is running by piecemeal; and buses in service are free of charge and looking like sardine cans. It is getting chilly. I get out of the house and head to Brighton Beach.

On my way down Surf Avenue, I bump into a group of young people struggling to communicate with Russian-speaking locals: Do you have power? Water? Food? Anybody need medical help? *Occupy Sandy.* Unevenly ripped tape is pasted on their jackets instead of name tags (Bill, Samantha, Sean), and their hands are loaded with legal pads, maps, and cell phones. They are definitely Park Slope types, and for a minute I feel like an indigenous Guatemalan woman patronized by an international NGO. (Park Slope, a middle-class neighborhood in downtown Brooklyn—shrinks, writers, academics—was generally unaffected by the storm except for a few collapsed trees and, in some places, a couple of hours of candlelight.) I introduce myself on behalf of the indigenous population and explain that in this complex, the condominium with a maintenance crew, we got back power and water quickly, in a matter of days. We all lost our cars, but this is a bourgeois problem, isn't it?

I can read fleeting puzzlement in their eyes. I sound more like them (people with bourgeois problems) and not like an indigenous woman. We got power, I repeat, but my mother, who lives in an old apartment building, still has no power or water. Neither does my friend Sasha, my uncle, and a few others in my surrounding who live in the neighborhood. They nod sympathetically. "Brighton Beach is NPZ,

No Power Zone," the leader, a tall handsome prince, says as he writes down names and addresses, adding that they have opened a help center nearby with supplies and water but unfortunately they can't help with power restoration. Landlords must pump the water out and electricians have to certify that the system is dry for Con Ed to switch them back on. "Are there older people you know stuck on high floors?" he asks, and mentions that National Guards are in the neighborhood.

Really? Better late than never, and I turn around the corner to West Fifth Street and West Brighton Beach, closed to traffic. Humvees and ambulances are flooding the intersection and paramedics and soldiers are running around and into the buildings, distributing water and blankets. Better late than never, I want to say to my mother, who has received a visit from the American Government, of which she wants less—and is offered less: bottled water on the tenth day and a nurse with a blood pressure contraption. She still has no power.

I continue on to Brighton Beach, maneuvering around piles of wet sand and mountains of black plastic garbage bags overflowing with spoiled cornucopia. Stores and restaurants are being emptied and the stench of decay is overwhelming. Almost all businesses are closed, but I spot one with light and walk through the doors. It is cold inside, but the herring and fresh homemade Russian *zakuski* (appetizers) are already there. A few freezing middle-aged saleswomen are behind the counter, stamping their feet and rubbing their hands, looking and sounding their usual Odessa selves. Pickles have just arrived, the red beet salad is fresh: "Berite, kushayte na zdorov'e!" (Please have some, enjoy!). Petya, the owner, unearthed some gas for the delivery, one of them adds with a conspiratorial wink. I congratulate them on rising from ashes so quickly; I was really craving those pickles.

Standing in the middle of the devastated immigrant paradise designated NPZ, I suddenly have a flashback of huge red letters hanging on a building across the Moscow River from the Kremlin: *Communism equals electrical + Soviet power, country-wide. V.I. Lenin.*

Chewing on my crunchy pickle produced without electrical but with plenty of capitalist power, I turn back home. Our parking lot, formerly the cemetery of cars, is now renamed Occupy GEICO Place. Indeed, the GEICO "catastrophe team" were our first responders, arriving here the day after the storm in cars and trailers. They set up office right in the parking lot, their RV equipped with satellite-powered laptops and printers. Car by car by car, within a few days, we the lucky GEICO-insured had our claims processed, cars totaled and towed away, and checks issued on the spot by friendly compassionate adjusters from Chicago, Georgia, and Florida.

For weeks to come, tow trucks will make sad trips back and forth, dragging away our Sandy-slain sputniks of comfort and freedom. Slowly but surely, new shiny cars will occupy the empty parking spots. Eventually, I too will have gotten myself a new cheerful red Hyundai with an appropriate name for an immigrant, *Accent*, jotted in optimistic silver letters on its hatchback.

This is America after all. I had been craving a new car.

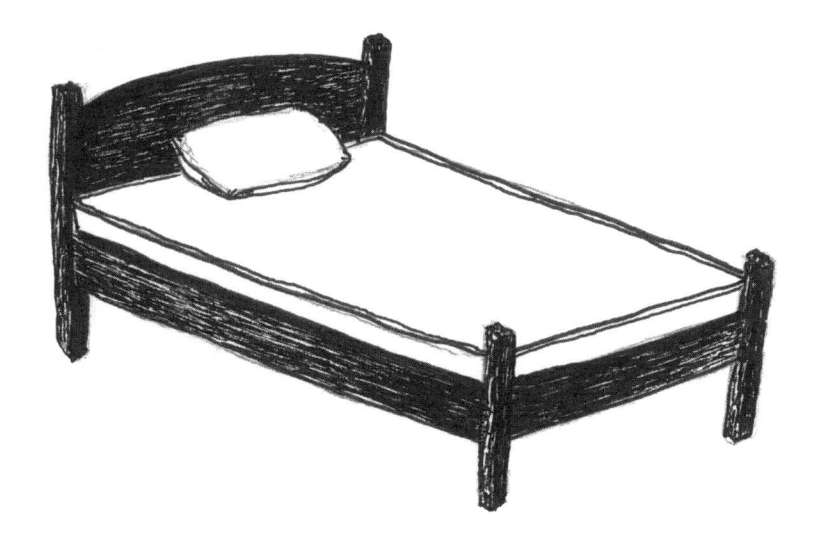

SAMUEL TOLZMANN   DRAWING MADE WHILE WAITING FOR MY HAIR TO GROW

DRAWING MADE WHILE WAITING FOR MY HAIR TO GROW

Sara Batkie

THOSE WHO LEFT AND THOSE WHO STAYED

The night the ground beneath Sherwood, Alaska split in two, the only witness to the tragedy was Kirby, the village drunk. It was mid-December, the kind of cold that cracks cloth. In summer the earth was damp and suckled at the townspeople's toes as they walked over it. But by winter it was brittle, temperamental, sharp as elbows. Everyone else was buried deep in their beds.

As the floe broke loose and began to float away carrying nine of them with it, Kirby slumped against a lamppost and watched the shoreline recede slowly into the darkness. No one, as usual, heard his hiccups.

They lost the lights first. Then the rest of the electricity followed. Three days in, they were storing perishable food outdoors. Kirby downed the remainder of his alcohol, stepped off the ice and into the sea. Two more tried to swim back to shore. Another vanished trying to find the other side of the floe in a storm. The five who remained moved on to the canned and dry goods. The youngest was seven, the oldest eighty-three, and the rest somewhere in between. Before they'd been neighbors. They weren't certain what they were now.

With no reception and all lines cut, most of them lost hope of getting in touch with the loved ones they'd left behind. But they held on to wild possibilities, of passing a steamer ship or getting picked up by a helicopter traveling overhead. Maybe a whale would swallow them whole, turn them into a colony of Jonah's. Or they'd plow right into another piece of land. Eventually the hope of being rescued or perishing in such ways dwindled too.

Lloyd, the town handyman, was the first to wake on the morning after the split. His immediate thought was to find his flashlight and shine it over the sea, in the hopes that someone would answer. He had a fiancée, Orya, back in the town. She'd been living with her parents until they could marry. Everyone agreed it was the respectable thing to do. But the glow was too slight to meet anyone; it disappeared into the jaundiced fog. Lloyd never realized how ugly the sky could be when it was all you saw.

The second thing he did was take a hatchet to his front door. He'd been building a raft ever since. He was a man who needed something to do with his hands.

When he and Orya first met, he had asked what her name meant and she said peace and that was what she would give him. This had been true for a time. But the last few weeks he'd been dreaming of other women's faces. It would happen unexpectedly, while he was sanding down a board, for instance. He'd bend over to pick up the stray curls and suddenly there was a woman beneath him, one he hadn't thought of for many years, her hair tangled in his fingers, her body warmer than anything for miles.

He couldn't think of his fiancée this way, though he wanted to. They had not yet known each other in the intimate sense. This was Orya's bidding; she was nineteen years old and, having waited this long, perhaps didn't see anything disagreeable in waiting a bit longer. Lloyd obliged because he was thirty-four and still somewhat surprised that she had agreed to know him at all.

He remembered her spider-leg eyelashes. How she read cookbooks all the way through like a novel. He thought how well she'd taken to his mother, Beulah, and feared what they spoke of without him there. He imagined her standing at the ocean's edge, in the wedding dress he hadn't yet seen her in. He wondered how long she would wait to leave him. That was when the others came in: the soft down belly of one, the violin bowed body of another. Moving beneath him, above him, and then wriggling out of sight, as they had in his life. He used to see them walking in town. They'd smile at him in that knowing, pitying way. Almost all of them married other people the year after they'd been with him.

Lloyd continued to build, taking the post office, the bar and its swinging saloon doors along the way. Though few words had passed between him and the others on the floe, it was assumed he would take them with him. The construction was slower than he hoped; he hadn't worked without electric tools since his apprentice days and the labor of it exhausted him.

Jude stopped by daily to check his progress and ask for firewood. The boy was seven and caught here with his mother Alicia, one of the many women from the cannery who mourned a husband that still lived. The boy must have sensed his fatigue because one day he invited Lloyd to have dinner at his mother's house. The offer touched him. He had never been entirely comfortable around children; they made his already hulking figure seem perilous. But on his way over that night, he caught a glimpse of Alicia undressing through her bedroom window, lit up by a pauper candle. Her belly was full and indulgent as a yawn but even from a distance he could see her skin had begun chipping like ice, the dark hoods that had settled under her eyes. As he watched, she slowly worked a comb through the ragged net of her hair. The somber beauty of it clanged his bones and rather than eat with this woman and her son, he turned back around and sent his ax through the door of the bookshop. The force of it rattled the pages that hadn't yet frozen together. Jude continued to visit him, but he never extended the invitation again.

Alicia was running out of food to feed her son. One morning it was six dry flakes of cereal in a milkless bowl. Would the next be sawdust? Milk from her own breast? If there were any animals, she'd hunt for them. But out here each crunch across the ice could echo for miles, a single step made seismic. It seemed they were alone.

Her son was not a good eater and in the past few weeks Alicia had been making a game of their meals, splitting up his food into real estate. Plots of peas, mashed potato complexes. But there was not enough here to make a single home. She'd already stopped eating just about anything herself.

"It's not good to skip breakfast," he told her once.

"I'm not hungry," she lied.

Jude reached across the table for her bowl, tipped his sideways, and parceled three flakes from one to the other. Then he pushed it back without a word. They ate them one at a time, letting the cereal melt into soggy cardboard on their tongues.

She tried to maintain some sort of normalcy with Jude, sending him off during the day to spend time with Ms. Kimball, the schoolteacher. She wished him to continue learning, even if it were things he wouldn't be able to use.

Her husband Espen had never put much stock in education. He'd dropped out of high school when his father died to take his place in the family whaling business. They married not long after Alicia graduated. In Sherwood there were two strains of romantic desperation: that of the young, to find someone, and that of the old who didn't. Divorce was rare but a match made wisely was rarer.

Espen was not a bad husband when he was there to be one. But his work often kept him from home and Alicia was unprepared for the loneliness that would come to blight her love. She spent her days working in the cannery, wearing the prints off her fingertips, and her nights knitting sleeves that never evolved into sweaters. When she slept she fantasized about the other men in the factory pasting mermaid-shaped labels onto her skin. When she laughed the mermaids shimmied like tattoos. Espen would crash through the door unannounced, the shock of salt in his beard, offering a vial of ambergris or an Inuit's soapstone sculpture, and Alicia would feel the surface of her heart split like a cold lake. She tore at the layers of his clothes as if she hardly believed the body underneath. When she had their child, she didn't know where to wire the news. Now they were both at sea though she suspected he wasn't trying to reach her. With so much more ocean to sail, he had no reason.

Drifting apart. What an inadequate way to describe people deciding to leave one another. As if all it took was going limp. And every night Alicia sat down at the table with Jude and neglected again to tell him. After so many days working in the factory, she had longed for such closeness with her child and now she didn't know what to do with it.

On the morning she and Jude split their flimsy breakfast, Alicia resolved to do better. She gathered herself into her warmest coat, went to the closet where her husband stored his things, and dug out his fishing line and tackle box. She hadn't been angling since she was a child but the howling of her stomach thwarted the demurrals of her head.

Alicia hadn't been outside in weeks; looking out over their limited land, the houses that were left seemed to huddle together against the wind. She wasn't certain how long she walked until she reached the floe's edge but it didn't seem enough. The ice simply dropped into the sea, like someone turning a corner. Today the waves were calm, a sort of dirty-dish gray, but she could recall the nights when the water sounded like it was preparing to knock on her door, vampirically awaiting an invite inside.

She must have sat there for hours, drawing the line through the water, casting and reeling nothing back. The lure bobbed about the surface like a child at play. She remembered the catches her father would return with, heaps of fish, the scales shining like treasure. Her mother would fry them in a pan with butter. They would freeze the rest until winter and roast them over the fire along with chestnuts. But this sea betrayed no life roiling beneath it. She was right: they were alone.

That night she dreamed again of the sea, the waves seething, parting, unhinging like a jaw, leaping up to swallow them whole. She woke in a flood of sweat. In the morning, she took something else from her husband's closet: a rope, which she instructed Jude to tie around his waist and attach to the front doorknob before he went outside. An old trick farmers used on their cattle in storms. She would not lose another man to these waters. Not yet.

Ms. Kimball was a teacher with no schoolhouse. For twelve years she had been teaching at Sherwood Junior High in a single room with twenty students, some of who would never take another class after hers. Every fall she gathered up her composition books, bundled her pencils, clapped her erasers clean. Every spring she counted down the days until she returned. The purpose had been ripped from her life. She feared what came next. She'd been lost like this before.

In Sherwood, there were those who left and those who stayed. That was all the town was. But Ms. Kimball was unique in that she had come to it. For a time after her arrival she had been the object of great speculation amongst the other residents. She was a woman whose smallness was often underlined by the children surrounding her; she stood out from the town like a lone nesting doll. Perhaps she was an escaped inmate on the lam. Or part of the witness protection program.

The truth was Ms. Kimball was fleeing nothing more mundane than the sort of depression that the wealthy cured with insurance-proof pills. When she was thirty-three and living in Santa Fe her fiancé left her for another teacher, a man who taught civics in a neighboring district. Several hours later she was found at the local grocery store, wandering the baking aisle, slitting the bags of sugar like throats. She was quietly asked not to return to school the next year.

In the first few days on the floe, Ms. Kimball attempted to adjust to her new isolation. She broke into the bookshop and stole all the Harlequin romances. She joined Kirby for a couple belts on the bottles while he was still with them. She went to Mr. Ruben, the elderly invalid she had never seen on dry land, and listened while he played his records. But flashes of her former gloom would visit her, urging her towards a darkness more absolute than night. When Alicia came to her, asking if she would tutor her son Jude, she accepted partly in the hope that the boy would keep something bad at bay.

Five weeks in Jude was beginning to look frail. Or at least she thought it was five weeks; she'd stopped crossing the days off her calendar once they'd passed the New Year.

On the walk over to Mr. Ruben's, hands clasped, stepping on the ice with the unpracticed gait of topiary come to life, Jude told Ms. Kimball of his wish to go to the moon.

"What's on the moon?"

"Don't know. It just seems weird up there. I'd like to go somewhere weird."

"More weird than this?"

It was strange to walk over land that stayed the same as far as the eye could see. It was what, as a child, she'd always imagined the clouds of heaven to look like. Yes, how different was this from the moon, really? They had about as much chance of being heard and even less of being believed. Then she stumbled over a rocky patch and gripped Jude tighter. Their hands were almost the same size.

They entered Mr. Ruben's house without knocking; he never answered anyway. His communication was rigid and tidy, restricted to gesture, the glottis, and his record player, old enough to be cranked by hand. He was a widower, had been for as long as Ms. Kimball had lived in Sherwood. They were there to keep him company and feed him, if he wanted it. Sometimes he did. Sometimes he let the soup dribble down his chin.

Mr. Ruben was in his chair, a mound of blankets at his feet that Ms. Kimball quickly picked up and arranged on his lap. It was colder here than it was outside. Around them the walls wolf-whistled, the clapboards stacked and gappy as unbraced teeth. A frost had formed on the kettle and it took several matches before she could get the stove gas to catch.

"I took a trip once," she said, pulling the kettle from its flame. "To India."

"Not possible," Jude said. This was what their lessons amounted to now: she told him of her life and he pretended to be interested.

"This was a long time ago. Before the floods came."

"What was it like?" Jude asked.

"Hot. Always hot. You couldn't get away from it, even in the shower. You couldn't really get away from anything. It's funny, now I can't even remember the last time I sweat."

She poured the boiled water into a mug and dipped a dusty tea bag inside, carrying it all to Mr. Ruben who didn't move to take it from her.

"Did you see any camels?"

"Once or twice. I saw all sorts of things: palaces, snake charmers, bodies laid out in the street. I watched a missionary perform an exorcism. I even bartered for a pair of sandals in bare feet once."

"Must have been sad to come back here," Jude said.

"Yes but it was necessary. Half the appeal of a journey is that it won't last. The way back is always shorter than the way there."

She lifted the mug to Mr. Ruben's lips and was rewarded with a hasty slurp. As she pulled away, she felt that old creeping unpleasantness she thought she'd left in New Mexico. Perhaps it was the talk of India. Perhaps it was the boy and his candlewick face. But she knew soon the creep would turn to a sprawl and she would do something cruel.

Jude heard once that there were places where animals were kept stuffed behind glass, twisted into poses that made them look like they did in life. He'd never seen it himself. His friend Freddie had gone on vacation and come back with tales of standing so close to beasts he could fog up the glass between them with his breath. It felt that way now, being stuck on this ice. But who was watching them? Maybe God, but Jude didn't know much about him either.

All his life he'd been dreaming of things he'd never seen. For as long as he could remember his dreams, he'd imagined stowing away in the hold of his father's ship and waking up on the same land he did. But now that a true adventure was at hand, he didn't know how to enjoy it.

Partly it was his mother, who was shrinking from the world in ways he didn't understand. He had always accepted her as beautiful, in the way women in fairy tales were beautiful; it was less about how she looked than how men held doors open for her or how his father used to gaze at her from across the kitchen table, a comical glint in his eye as if contemplating this plank of wood that kept him from the woman he'd crossed an ocean for. Now her growing weakness frightened and angered Jude. He knew it wasn't her fault, but who else could he blame? Every morning when he pushed half of his cereal towards her, his resentment, a feeling he knew but couldn't name, thickened.

Six weeks on, one of Jude's teeth came loose. He was poking a finger through a hole in his favorite shirt, trying to tickle himself, when his tongue lifted his front incisor from its root. It hung suspended for a moment then flapped back into place. This didn't concern him immediately; he'd lost teeth before. But this one was full grown. His father had pulled it from his mouth over a year ago.

Before leaving the yard, he tied the rope around his waist and attached the other end to the front doorknob. As he picked his way over the bald expanse of ice, the growls of his stomach were matched by the whip of the wind, snow enveloping his footprints as soon as he planted them. The rope flopped behind him like a misplaced cowlick.

Jude enjoyed these excursions despite their difficulty. On his seventh birthday his father had promised to enroll him in the Cub Scouts. Jude began making his bed drum tight every morning. Once or twice his mother humored him by bouncing a quarter off it. That summer she'd even let him sleep outdoors, draping a sheet over a low-hanging branch to make a pup tent. He traced the stars out with his fingers, dreaming of the day he'd know their names. But that was almost four months ago and he hadn't seen his father since. He didn't know the stars any better either, though he saw them more clearly out here; they seemed closer too, as if the sky was sinking.

Halfway on his journey he stopped to say hello to Lloyd, who was outside working on his raft. The rope followed behind, nipping at Jude's ankles like a dog.

"How is it?" he asked. He still hadn't gotten used to speaking easily with Lloyd. The man's mammoth presence and quiet manner had always frightened Jude; he took up space without warning. But now Jude was glad Lloyd was with them.

"Not bad," Lloyd said, stepping back from the plane of wood as if to admire it. "Think it could hold about seventy stone."

"How many stones do you need?"

"Don't know. How much is your mother weighing these days?" His mouth was smiling but his eyes were limp.

Jude didn't knock before entering Ms. Kimball's house, a lapse in propriety that made him feel oddly adult. She called out his name from the living room, as if it could be anyone else. The sound of it bounced off the bare walls. A few weeks ago there'd been a painting in the foyer, a woman with dark skin, long braids, and no clothes, but after Jude asked about it, it disappeared.

In the living room he hesitated to approach the woman sprawled out on the couch. Her face was tucked into the crook of her arm, her breath straining to escape her. She reminded him of a man he'd once seen while walking in the woods with Freddie. The man had hair like knotty black string and fingernails long enough to curl. His eyes couldn't seem to settle on anything. He wore a bracelet on his wrist, white and plastic, and when Freddie stepped on a branch as they ran away, they heard him let out a low moan. That night, the police swept the area but Jude never came across him again. Ms. Kimball looked like that man, except he actually knew her, which made it all the more frightening.

"Do you think the ocean ever gets tired?" she mumbled into her hand. "It's been going since the world began, you know?"

Jude didn't quite know how to respond to an adult who wasn't looking at him.

"Always carrying the rest of us on its back," she continued. "Where do you think it's taking us now?"

"Home?"

"What home? Maybe Siberia. We can be prisoners too."

"I want to go home," Jude said.

She turned on him then, the thorny mass of her hair, her uninhabited eyes, her jaw wound tight like a music box before it sings. She looked poised to pounce and Jude jumped backward, stumbling over an unplugged lamp cord.

"Go then, what's stopping you? Nothing, that's what. There's nothing there."

"My father's there."

"Your father left your mother months ago. That means he left you too."

"No," Jude shouted. In the hurry to get the word out, he almost pushed the tooth loose.

"No?" Ms. Kimball said. "Ask her. Just ask her. Nobody's there. Nobody's anywhere."

Then she deflated like a balloon, collapsing back into the couch in a silent heap. Jude watched her for a moment, his pulse jangling in his head, a fire building in his fingertips. He glanced at the cord at his feet, the lamp attached to it, and the rope attached to him, coiled on the floor like Eden's snake. Then he turned around and ran.

The wind hit him like a bear hug, a huge enveloping gush of air that almost pushed him back into Ms. Kimball's house. For a moment he saw nothing and felt a surge of blind, furious hope. But when his sight returned he still saw nothing. Just white upon white upon white. It buried whatever else he was feeling.

Lloyd was not at the raft but the ax was. Jude didn't lift it so much as throw himself behind it. The blade ripped through the wood, sending splinters raining through the air. The tooth was knocked from its socket with the effort and as he spit it into the snow, a jerky piano rang across the hill. And then a voice tiptoeing over it. Mr. Ruben had put a record on. *Baby, won't you please come home.* The same record every night. With the taste of blood like a penny on his tongue, Jude readied himself for the next blow.

The boy would be forgiven. Boys always were. Until they were men and not so easily worthy. Then old age came and they could be pardoned again. Mr. Ruben would know. He'd been them all, once.

Mr. Ruben had lived every one of his eighty-three years in Sherwood. Some he remembered better than others. Since the death of his wife Zuleika eleven years before he'd been trying to forget the rest. Not that he had loved her so very well. Mr. Ruben was a man who always thought hard about being better. He just never seemed to find the time to do it.

The year Mr. Ruben was born was the hottest on record. This excited his parents who believed it portended something great for their son. Then it kept happening year after year. A new record, a new disappointment, and soon enough, a new everything.

Here's what he understood about the boy: there was a great confusion to being young, a frenzy that most adults were more than happy to forget. Every single thing was the biggest yet. His own memories of those days were culled objects, like a museum show of his own making. There was the bucket his mother used for fresh well water. If he drank directly from the ladle, he received a scolding. It must be poured into a glass instead, the liquid so clear and sharp it popped when it hit his tongue. He remembered his first and only lobster, its hard red shell and the sound of it splitting, like a bad word you couldn't take back. Watching his father shoot a reindeer and two weeks later, giving his mother the pelt for Christmas.

He watched the town sputter through history, growing and receding and going gray. Every few years another upheaval: the fishing industry failing, the young people migrating, the winters colder and shorter, feral and blunt, the summers hanging on like bated breath. As a child he'd been taught that March was in like a lion, out like a lamb, that April showers brought May flowers, but such sayings dropped out of use by the time he was in high school—they no longer met the needs of the new world. And yet he lived a life not much different from that of his parents: he married young, worked until he was sixty, haphazardly raised children of his own. If they were occasionally wanting for something, there were always neighbors to help. The things he was used to having he eventually got used to doing without.

Since Zuleika had passed, he'd stopped listening to anything aside from his records; he read no news and heard from no one. So perhaps the town's misfortune had been inevitable. Perhaps they'd stayed too long in a place they shouldn't. It had surprised but not alarmed him to wake up one morning floating on ice. And though he did feel bad for the young people, he couldn't help being delighted at this last excitement of his life. He had expected to drift off into the ether of old age; now he would meet a great and unusual end. He spent every day with salt kinking his nostrils and the current beneath his feet, tugging him further into a world muted enough to write his last wishes on. He didn't have many.

The teacher had promised to stay with him. For years he'd exploited his own deficiencies, allowed everyone to believe he was worse off than he was. The world in his head had always seemed better than anything anyone else offered. Perhaps for her he could lay the charade aside.

Here's what else Mr. Ruben understood: life was a series of big moments and by the end, you could forget every one. Each night when he nestled into his chair and put the needle down onto his Bessie Smith record, he did not think of Zuleika or his children or the town he'd left behind. Instead he saw a darkness, much like the one that surrounded him now, and two friends he hadn't seen in many years, boys again as was he. They had smuggled themselves over to the house of their history teacher, Ms. Ratched, and were lifting one another to look into her window. The others had come back down with nothing to report but when he had his turn, she was there, stark naked, standing in the middle of the room. Her body was taut and still slick with water, the skin stretching over her like a grape's. A cigarette dangled from her fingers, the ash floating carelessly into the carpet. And over by the unmade bed, a pair of black high heels awaiting her return. The three of them squealed and ran together, and it seemed in that moment that there was nowhere they couldn't go.

On the morning they pushed the raft from the floe, a fog unrolled itself over the ocean. Lloyd could barely see his own hand in front of him but he didn't think that would keep them from getting somewhere. It had taken another two weeks to repair the damage that Jude had done. It might have taken less if his mother hadn't made him help, sulking while he drove the same nails into the same plane of wood. They were huddled together somewhere nearby though Lloyd couldn't see them either. They'd grown so thin the wind must have been cutting through them like clothes on a line.

Neither Ms. Kimball nor Mr. Ruben came to see them off. Lloyd expected this. But Mr. Ruben didn't play a record for them either. This disappointed him. Now that they were going, he could admit it might be the last song he ever heard.

As the floe became a mound and then a white line and then an inkling, a fear gripped him, coarse but not unpleasant. A fear like presents at Christmas. A fear like something coming apart in space. A fear like the day when he was twelve and running along the edges of Sherwood with his friends and was the first to see it: a whale, beached on the open palms of the land. The scent of fish heads and formaldehyde was in the air. Even from a distance they could tell it was still breathing; they watched the labor of it work across its body. It was gray as Guernica. But they were young and selfish and kept it a secret. Two days later it had grown solid with death and yet no more real. They went closer and then closer until it was big as an eclipse. They dared one another to be the first to touch it. Lloyd was the second; it was damp as a fevered forehead but without the relief of warmth. In the end the National Guard had to airlift out the corpse via helicopter. No one had seen a creature on shore since.

There could be no music waiting for them. There could be nothing at all.

But as the sea bent beneath them, a beat entered his brain: Orya, he thought, Orya. And whatever hopes were in the heads of the others joined him in turn. It became the current they were crossing.

Sue Landers

THEY WILL EXIST EVEN WHEN THEY WON'T, OR, THIS THEN WILL BE A DESCRIPTION OF THAT THING

Before the street with the house where a phone rang wasn't named for anyone it was named for a house named for a place named for a person named Loudoun.

A house on a hill. A house where no one lived. A house without a story. A story few have told. A house with no history. A house with some history. A house with no particular history but is picturesque and ancient.

Long before it was a house without a story Loudoun was a house full of people with names repeating like things like family and built for a merchant named Armat who had things like streets named after him. Armat had children named Sara and Jane.

Sara was not of sound mind. She spoke in broken sentences. It was difficult for her to form sentences. It was difficult for her to form ideas. She would put her finger in the corner of her eye and utter some ideas she had formed. When she came of age her father's father who shared her name and a man named Skerrett took her money away.

When Jane came of age she married her cousin who shared her name but who died like her father so she married Skerrett a banker who liked to buy furniture. Together they bought lots of furniture for their house in the country named Loudoun.

Then Jane and Skerrett had a daughter named Anna who married a man whose father's father's father was a Logan. The Logan who knew so much about books he told Ben Franklin which books to put in his library. And the two of them together Anna and the Logan were not very happy.

He left her alone and she kept track of his comings and goings. She kept track of the days he left her alone with their children. The days he left her for drink or the maid. Then she left him and she kept all her money. She left him and got some of his. Somehow she managed this he must have been a monster.

And after the two of them died two of their children lived in the house without talking and they took pictures of all of their things. They took pictures of their parlor and the bedroom and the fireplace and the hemlock. They took pictures of the hickory and their specimen marble table. They took pictures of their paintings their chairs and of their chandelier. They took pictures of their dog. Their dog named Beautiful Witch.

Then the last living one of the family whose name she no longer had died. Then the last living one named Maria gave the house to the city. She gave the house to the city where it sat. Where it sat with its things and its pictures of things. The galloons and the fringe the socks and the sheets and the shoes.

After Maria died there was a war. And a distant relation a Logan who liked the histories of things like family and houses used the house to collect things for the war. This distant relation liked her family's place in history she liked things. And she and the ladies she invited to the house collected things in the house for the war.

Then the war ended and the house and its things went back to their sitting. A caretaker sat with its things with the lamps and the linens the plates and the harp the diaries the paintings and the fabrics.

Then a woman arrived a woman in pearls a woman looking for a cause who redecorated. Who moved things around the house as she liked. She liked the people who had used all the things she liked Anna so much she took her diary. She took the diary where Anna described her husband and what he did to her. She took the diary that Anna wrote in French like a code. She took the diary and hid it and no one knows where it is.

This woman this friend invited people to the house. But people rarely came. The people nearby didn't care for the house or its things. The people far away didn't care for the people nearby. So people didn't come and the house sat with its things. With its harp in the window. And the galloons and the fringe in the attic.

It was around this time that I came to know the house not its people. I came to know the house as a house on a hill without a history without people. A house in a park where my siblings looked for their things after their things were stolen by thieves.

And the house became increasingly vulnerable. Its caretakers wrote about break-ins. About people tearing up bricks from its lovely brick walk about ripping up bricks and throwing them. The caretakers wanted protection from vandals from thieves the neighbors. They wanted money for pendants they could wear around their necks they wanted pendants that would transmit their panic. They wrote letters describing it. About a situation one can't understand unless one is associated with it.

Then later the house was struck by lightning that caused a fire. Many things are believed to have been destroyed in the fire. Some things remain in places unknown. This is because the house and the things are still considered vulnerable so some people don't want to talk about it. Some things remain in archives and are documented.

Some of the things that remain are portraits. Of the family a portrait of Anna a sampler. And a folding needle case a needle case a friendship needle pincushion. Plates. Tongs a saucer with a figure holding a sword three cans and a saucer a sauce boat a small tea cup with saucer a saucer a soup plate.

Soup plate soup plate cup and saucer saucer two plates and a bowl. Two cups and a saucer a bowl with flower swags a plate broken in half and repaired. Soup bowl soup bowl soup bowl soup bowl a soup bowl broken in two pieces a charger. A charger a shell-shaped dish a round scalloped-edge bowl a round scalloped-edge bowl a deep scalloped bowl an oval dish with scalloped edge. Sauce tureen sauce tureen and matching ladle saucer for a sauce tureen saucer for a sauce tureen footed bowl or compote. Dog figurine a cream pitcher. Charger charger charger charger silhouette pistol. A box of assorted marble samples. A silhouette of a lady with hair ribbons. One specimen marble table.

And a Grecian wine cup

A skyphos

From the second half of the 4th century

BCE.

Casey Wiley

PLANTATION, FLORIDA

(Names have been changed to protect privacy.)

2003: The day I moved into a rented room in a 1960s ranch-style house in a middle class neighborhood in Plantation, Florida, my landlord Debbie's on-again, off-again boyfriend, Pete, a crispy-tanned forty-something guy who could have passed for Richard Gere's brother (the face holding an occasional smirk and he had squinted eyes, puffy brushed back graying hair), a guy who worked at a golf course maybe forty miles north and spoke with a pronounced Panhandle drawl, he moved (back) into the house in the morning, got drunk in the afternoon and attempted to make scratch pasta for the three of us for supper.

We ate Kraft mac & cheese at a plastic table on the patio by the pool. Pete and Debbie puffed cigarettes and made a big deal about blowing smoke away from me.

In her late forties, Debbie was an anxious, chain-smoking, unemployed legal aid in Ft. Lauderdale. Her skin tanned like a cowboy boot, its color was offset by her usual attire of neon cotton t-shirts and shorts. She laughed a lot and she coughed a lot. Her parents had died recently, but it was unclear how recently. The furniture in the house was a clear 70s style. Lime green chairs. All-white carpet. An open-topped white piano that no one played sat in a corner of the living room. She said most of the stuff had been her parents. She liked it? Did I like it? she'd say. Oh, I didn't have to like it, she'd say. I like it, I'd say, maybe sitting on her fifteen-foot white couch. It's unique, I'd say. Her dining room table was covered completely in glass bowls and pitchers that she said she'd get around to putting away soon. Dozens of silver and pewter kitchen objects—bowls, saucers, little plates—were strewn across her living room floor. Stuff Debbie said—as she sat out at that plastic table by the pool—that she was going to polish. When she had a moment.

Then she'd light another cigarette, stare up at the dark night.

Plantation is a suburb six miles west of Ft. Lauderdale. Black Olive, Mahogany, Yellow Tabebuia, Gumbo Limbo trees tower in many of the neighborhoods, their branches forming great canopies over some streets. (Hurricane Wilma in 2005, and other tropical storms, toppled many of these trees.) Then just outside of Debbie's neighborhood: Strip malls and condo villages with names like Cape Sunset and Palm Grove. Everything flat, at sea level, give or take, and few buildings with basements. (Flooding worries.) Four-lane megastreets with traffic lights at every corner. Fast food, day spas, bars, golf courses and massage parlors. Palm trees and palm plants in planters and bus stops with benches that double as advertisements for attorneys and plastic surgeons. Bright yellow houses and neon green houses and squat, all-glass business buildings. When I think of the area, the term "pink stucco" comes to mind. When my sister visited from Seattle she pointed out that there were no sidewalks. Walking anywhere outside of neighborhoods was nearly impossible.

The humidity was like an inescapable memory.

Debbie said she put the room up for rent because she was out of work and needed the $400, though I surmised pretty quickly that any companionship, even my rarely-there-not-a-great-talker-kinda-tired-want-to-go-to-bed kind, seemed to be worth at least half that to her. The room I rented might've doubled for a $150-budget stage interpretation of how Heaven might look, if Heaven were a tacky white bedroom. Wall-to-wall very white carpet. A king-sized bed that took up about 80 percent of the floor space. An old dial TV in the corner. A closet, and a teal padded 70s loveseat. I tried reclining on it to read, which meant leaning on my side against its one sloped armrest like maybe a silent movie actress might do when posing for a picture, but this never felt comfortable. Instead I set my laptop on the loveseat, intending to use it as a tiny desk. I'd kneel on the white carpet and try to type fiction.

A few weeks before, I had graduated college in upstate New York, not far from my home in the Adirondacks. I was now in South Florida as an intern for the Miami Dolphins, which entailed working 70 hour grunt-work weeks: I helped a guy run youth football clinics at area elementary schools, though I was as much a football player as Pee Wee Herman was a power lifter; I typed stuff into computers; when the front desk lady, Ruby, wasn't there, I manned the front desk and answered the phone (could a fan meet a player?); I buzzed players driving tinted window SUVs into their parking lot; when the mail guy, Mark, wasn't there, I sorted mail; I stocked drink coolers with water, soda, and Gatorade; I lined practice fields with white spray paint; sweated—and when I wasn't working, I was either watching bad TV on my end of Debbie's house or I was trying not to be home. Late at night in generic coffee shops in strip malls around Plantation and Davie and Sunrise I wrote rambling stories about lonely protagonists.

CASEY WILEY PLANTATION, FLORIDA

Maybe a month into living in the Florida house, early in the morning as I was microwaving a frozen chicken burrito, Debbie told me that Pete—who, when not working at the golf course, which seemed to be most days, spent his time watching daytime talk shows in bed—she told me that Pete was an alcoholic, but after some thought, after *a lot* of thought, she said, she was giving him a chance and would let him stay in the house. He promised to sober up. I said thanks for telling me, that Pete was a good guy. She asked if I really thought so. He was funny, I remember thinking, goofy, harmless, a guy who seemed to like sitting around. I must have taken too long to answer because then Debbie told me that her brother, who lived a few hours north, was a meth addict, and that he needed help. Not that I could help him, she said. But she wanted me to know. Because I'm part of the house now, she said. I said thanks and that I hoped he'd get better, or you know, whatever he needed, but despite this intimate news, I was thinking about how it felt weirdly good that she said I was a part of this home, 70s furniture and struggles and all.

She said he might visit soon, her brother, just so I know.

Then she told me that he was dying.

From a distance, initially, the football job seemed miraculous to me. Despite being a book guy, an English major, I'd been a Dolphins fan for years (Dan Marino was right up there with Carver, Hemingway and Tim O'Brien), and despite having figured out that the interns made about two bucks an hour, my bosses, tough talking guys, made the job—as piddling as it was—they made the job feel like it was the most important thing in the world: They had all been interns and look at them now. They were guys in pressed slacks and polo shirts with a small dolphin on them. And I was happy to go along with that. Cause look at where I was: This beautiful facility! Pow! Yes! Players and coaches and cheerleaders! Despite my below-janitor status, I felt strangely important there, on the inside. This glossy idea of the job spilled into the idea of South Florida, South Beach, the Clevelander, neon, skin, sand and no shoes, perpetual summer. But despite this perceived glitz, and the shine on polished football helmets, it sounds silly now, but I missed my college friends and—nerd!—the college lit. magazine staff I had worked with, my family ... and Debbie had a way of getting me to talk about that. She made it feel like all this wasn't a big deal, that I shouldn't keep stuff pasted to the inside of my chest. She'd catch me passing through the living room, avoiding pewter or silver bowls, and she'd say, I've got a minute, Case, and she'd sit out at that table and listen. I still had this new/cool job glow then, so I told her about the work I did and about working hard and how people at the Dolphins, high-up people, started where I was and moved up to big-shot positions with the team. That the team VP started as an intern in equipment, washing jock straps. And maybe that could be me? And, and, and.

"Are you happy, Case?" she said on one of those nights. (I quote because those are exactly her words.) What? I said. Yes, I said. Yes.

Debbie had lived in Ft. Lauderdale most of her life and seemed to have floated right along with the lifestyle that accompanies the once famous "Ft. Liquordale" moniker. She told me she worked as a legal aid "and partier" (her words) for twenty years. She'd recount trysts with Ft. Lauderdale attorneys, about guys who had lined up to propose, but at the end of the day—or night!—she'd say that she'd always turned them away. So she never married, wore that like one might a tattoo from a decade back; she wasn't boasting, but she was confident in her decision. She couldn't commit, she said. She'd liked her freedom. Debbie was a good-looking lady, pretty in a cheesy Florida way. A-few-too-many-cigarettes–too-few-meals thin, dyed blond hair, dark roots and a nice smile. Decent teeth. An easy laugh. Most of what she said, no matter the gravity, was followed by a smile or chuckle. She was smart, up on the news and local politics and she had an endearing way of making fun of herself: Oh look at me, she'd say. I've worn this outfit all week! Looking down at her neon shorts, her tennis shoes, she'd laugh, snort (also endearing) but it's not like she was self-conscious enough, or cared enough, to go inside and change. She was cool with all this, for now: just chillin' out, looking across the pool, smoking, occasionally chuckling to herself. She had a series of girlfriends who all seemed to be forever single and looking, living in suburban homes like Debbie's. Occasionally they'd come by for drinks, dressed in white cotton pants or shorts and flowing white tops. Tan, baked skin from years in the sun. They'd smoke out by the pool and cackle and recount and tell me that I wouldn't want to hear their stories, and then they'd tell me anyway. I think they were all named Kathy.

Three-or-so months into living at Debbie's house, her brother visited for a couple days and stayed with us. He was very small, a head shorter than Debbie, with the body of a twelve-year-old with a gut, and he dressed in long denim shorts and billowing airbrushed t-shirts. Flat-brimmed baseball cap worn askew, pronounced gold chain. Debbie said he had his own style; he was basically one of those white gangsta'/wangsta' guys. Judging by Debbie's age and that he was her "younger brother," I assumed he was about forty, but he looked fifty-five. He didn't say much. The only thing he and I talked about was his pacemaker, and we talked about this for maybe three minutes. Out by the pool he told me he wore big t-shirts to conceal it. He sweated profusely, outside in the South Florida heat and inside in the air conditioning. He also referred to a girlfriend as if she were with him, although I never saw her, and she seemed to never be at Debbie's house. From what Debbie told me, her brother spent much of the visit at a local outdoor flea market a few miles north of Debbie's place. It was the size of a fairground, Debbie said. China sets and books and croquet mallets and art, she said. Anything you can imagine. I imagined dry, fine dirt getting kicked up all over the place, and curled sneakers and shoes stacked on tables and lots of velvet paintings of Elvis and pensive looking Native Americans. And this small man (determined? lonely?) drifting through all that. Have you been there? Debbie said. I've driven by, I said. All day, she said, her brother'd spend all day wandering the aisles looking for god knows what.

A few nights a week, despite my usual late returns home, I'd end up drinking a beer out at the table on the patio with Debbie. It was easy to get engulfed in the macho, non-stop work atmosphere of the football job, but Debbie would remind me of real life; she thought my job was absurd, and often told me so. She saw through the perceived teal and orange glamour; slave labor, she called it, with a grin. She'd ask about my typical day and chuckle as I recounted getting up at five, getting home at nine. She could never get enough of that; she'd ask me my schedule like a person would ask another to repeat a favorite joke. When I told her I was even working all-night security at the team facility a few times a month, then staying at work the next day to do my "day job," she'd howl. Actually fall back in her chair.

At first this made me mad; for a while I liked living a double life: football guy talking and sweating football all day, and then this nerd at night donning glasses and hanging in coffee shops and the chain bookstore down the street. Maybe I needed both lives. But maybe Debbie was right. This once glitzy idea—my Florida life, the team, this perpetual summer—was beginning to wrinkle, while the front-of-my-face reality became that very white bedroom in Debbie's house, that pool, that plastic table and Debbie smoking cigarettes and chuckling long into the night. She was the only person there who I'd talk to about stuff unrelated to football, which sometimes meant the occasional writing I was doing.

Debbie said the only thing she wrote was shopping lists. Else she'd be too scared to see what she'd get on paper. We were quiet then, as I remember, watching the pool.

I never saw Debbie use the pool. I used it twice, once when my sister visited and once when Debbie was gone for about a week. But she loved that pool. I imagined she called it her own little ocean, her little sparking ocean, but I don't think she called it anything.

Pete came and went, a coastal breeze. Debbie never seemed to fight too hard to keep him around; sometimes it seemed it was her decision for him to go. He and I never talked much, but when he got going, he'd roll. He'd tell me stories about growing up in the Panhandle, stories about his year in college, drunken stories. Debbie would laugh along, or phase out, sitting quietly. The silver and pewter bowls remained strewn on the living room floor, glass pitchers and bowls on the dining room table. Debbie said she should get around to applying for jobs. Money's getting low, she'd say, chuckling. I realized then that the chuckle was her way of undercutting or maybe softening the statement: about a job, about money, about her family, about Pete. At my lowest, my most sleep-deprived, I thought she verged on being nuts. (How could she sit around all the time, just staring off and smiling to herself?), and I know she thought I was crazy, working my skin off, running in place, too self-declared busy and/or self-absorbed to accept that I was unhappy. (Working for what?) We should have fought, bickered more, blamed the other, but we rarely did. It's total cheese, but I know I needed Debbie and I think at times she was glad I was around. I like to believe that combined, we would equal a normal person, maybe hair askew, a person that would blend in with any crowd.

About seven months into living in Florida, Debbie woke me up sobbing. 4 a.m. She was wearing a huge Van Halen tee-shirt that slipped off one of her shoulders. She was shaking her arms out frantically as if she couldn't feel her hands. Her brother—the one with the pacemaker, the maybe-meth-addict, the flea market enthusiast—was dead, she told me, her brother was dead: heart attack or suicide or drugs, or some combination. He was dead, he was dead. Died in his sleep—someone found him in his bed. Pete wasn't around. Here, then gone. This time he'd been gone for a couple weeks; I didn't know why, and I didn't ask. I sat with Debbie in the living room, a pile of silver bowls for maybe holding candy at my feet, as she called people on the phone (the Kathys?), and then outside at that plastic table so she could smoke, and after a while, because I was up, I went to work.

Debbie was gone for about a week. At some point Pete showed up. We ate pizza on the patio and talked about everything that did not matter in the world: the Dolphins' disappointing win loss record, golf courses, his car and its gas mileage—over thirty? wow—the weather. Yep, it was hot. Boy, yeah. It was at this moment, the both of us aware of the grass-blade-thin depth of our conversation, but chugging ahead anyway, strangers in the night, I understood that despite absconding from and jilting Debbie, this fragile bird, that I really liked Pete. His was real struggle that he'd attempt to aw-shucks off. He was tacky, crass, though nonjudgmental, and he never seemed to take himself too seriously (though from a distance this seems his ultimate malfunction). Like a little country kid, he never seemed to wear a shirt; Pete was chest out and proud of it despite being melanoma crispy looking—that tan, fragile layer, this masculine or beautiful or healthy (mis)perception of paradise stretching across his bones and muscle and soul—this real, packaged-up stuff ... this seemed pretty much as good a metaphor for South Florida as I've encountered.

Pete hung out in bed flipping channels for about twenty-four hours, then left.

One night that week, after coming home late from work, the house quiet and empty, I changed into trunks and swam in the pool. I kept the lights off on the patio and swam under the moon. The water was warm; it was always warm. I'd be leaving soon, I knew that. I'd had a few phone interviews back in the northeast, but there was no job lined up. Despite feeling exhausted, I couldn't sleep that night, my body a dead log, my head a carnival, and I thought about writing this down, laying out what I thought loneliness felt like, being in the wrong place—or the right place at one time—what that felt like. It felt like this: feeling miscast like I had tried out for the wrong part and—whoops—had gotten it, and this was trite in a could-be-worse-oh-Dolphins-what-an-opportunity sort of way, but despite that, the feeling was real. I had been playing a version of myself, been called the wrong name for months, but it's as if I hadn't the stones to tell the person that it wasn't my name. It's like I'd shrugged and started believing it was my name, this other name.

I lay awake for hours.

A few days later I got home from work early to see Debbie and Pete, the latter shirtless, in the garage struggling with a king-sized mattress. I asked her how she was doing. She said okay, laughed, shook her head, as I remember, and responded. This was my brother's, she said, meaning the mattress. It's almost new, she said. It'll be perfect for your bed. I said the mattress on the bed now was already great. That we should put this new mattress—her brother's mattress—in the guest room. For her friends (the Kathys), if they'd like to stay over. (They never did.) Or for out of town friends? Nonsense, Debbie said. We want you to use this. Pete'll Febreze it and we'll bring it in tomorrow.

The next night I slept on the floor in my room. And the next and the next and the next. One night I woke up wrapped in my sheet on the strip of white carpet between the bed and that teal loveseat, stared up at the ceiling for a while and finally crawled into the bed and slept.

A few weeks later Debbie went back to work. Pete had been at the house since that day with the mattress. Debbie said he hadn't had a drink since then. He was pale and lay around in bed quietly, but he usually made it to work anyway. He told me he was doing alright and I think he really meant it.

A couple weeks later, I moved back north.

Six years after leaving Florida and many jobs later, my fiancé-now-wife, Rachael, and I stayed for three weeks at a friend of a friend's house in Falls Church, VA that was being de-/reconstructed around us. I got a temporary job teaching English at a program for high school kids from rough family situations. The house was getting fixed up to be put on the market, and the friend of a friend who owned the house moved with his new wife to a house a few miles away. He mentioned that some guys would be coming by to paint and fix a few things.

Three guys who told me they were from El Salvador showed up every morning as I'd leave the house to go to my job. They were really nice and I think were confused why Rachael and I were there and they were apologetic, but I tried to be more apologetic, so we'd all end up in the kitchen saying sorry a lot and doing squeeze-against-the-counters dances around each other. They stripped all the wallpaper and repainted, redid the kitchen: sun roof, shiny new appliances. All the furniture was covered in white sheets, a house of ghosts at night. Rachael and I stayed in the guest bedroom one night, another bedroom the next, whichever room wasn't being remade at that moment. The place reeked of new paint. Early every morning we'd pack up our stuff and cram it in the trunk of our car to make sure it didn't get put away in storage. I felt stupid and helpless, a squatter; we should have gotten a hotel room even though the friend of a friend insisted we stay. But we didn't have much money. We'd never had much money.

Having dumped myself into another person's life, wandering inside their walls, pooping in their toilet, finding their notes on little scraps of paper on the nightstand, staring late one night at family photos on a wall, I thought of Debbie, whom, since leaving I'd talked with on the phone once and seen once. It's tricky for me, then, now, looking back, to recall my thinking at eighteen, nineteen, working at that football job, sitting alone late nights in strip mall coffee shops or out by Debbie's pool. How did I see my future self? A blur? Alone? Does it walk parallel to me now? And would I recognize that version of me? I tried to write about this self-absorbed sense of self in a story, working on the friend of a friend's bed, surrounded by dresser ghost and floor-lamp ghost, but the story went nowhere.

I did remember this, though: On a road trip I took in the southeast with my sister about eighteen months after I had left Florida, we stopped to see Debbie. We drank iced tea at that plastic table by the pool. She had a little bird then, her buddy, I think a parakeet that would perch on her shoulder and say things like "Hello!" and make throaty warbling noises. So she said "Hello!" a lot to the bird. And we said "Hello!" a lot to the bird. Debbie had gotten a legal aid job at a firm in Ft. Lauderdale. Lots of research, grunt work, she said. She really needed that drink at night! She told us Pete was no longer living with her. She didn't say how long he'd been gone.

Standing in her driveway in the late afternoon heat, we said goodbye. As Katherine and I were getting in our car, Debbie's neighbor, a big man, Latino, dark skinned and sweating—who I guess was my neighbor when I lived there, but whom I had never met—ran at us from his house across the street. He was holding a baby, small like Debbie's bird. He wore a pale green t-shirt that had a stretched neckline. Screaming: "Who knows CPR?" His little girl had stopped breathing! he yelled. She had been playing with her older sister out back and she'd swallowed something! he yelled. I called 911 on my cell phone. In the middle of the street, we reached awkwardly and tentatively for the baby in his arms, but the man wouldn't let her go. What would we do with her anyway? Her tiny face screamed, those scrunched eyes and pink open mouth, a mouth of longing and, yes, many future words, yes, her mouth, but there was no sound. The man was crying and yelling and he moved quickly to his lawn in a crouched run. My sister and I ran around and pounded on doors for someone who maybe he trusted. No one seemed to be home. Then we waited, Katherine, Debbie, her bird, and me, in a semicircle on the neighbor's lawn. The man laid his daughter carefully in the Bermuda grass. She was pale and small on the lawn. Her toes curled. We semi-knelt with him, semi-held-out our arms, stupidly helpless, watching this struggling little thing. Kneeling, he pushed lightly on her stomach, then her chest, and per my sister's suggestion, he lifted her gently and knocked lightly on her back.

A little girl, maybe five years old, messy pigtails, presumably the sister, emerged from around the house and walked tentatively across the yard, small steps, small steps, and Debbie stood up and waited for her. Debbie didn't use her name; maybe she didn't know it. But Debbie said it was okay, to the sister, that it was okay, little girl. The girl leaned stiffly into Debbie's arms. The bird made noise here and there. Debbie held the girl. From his knees, bending close to the baby's tiny mouth, the neighbor said he thought he could feel faint breath! Bending again, he said nothing. He whispered something into her chest, dropped tears on her naked chest. A man's big tears on a baby's papier-mâché chest. He cried loudly and then silently as he looked up the street for the ambulance. I glanced from the tiny girl to the street, back to the girl, Debbie's bird chirping, chirping, until the ambulance arrived and took the father and daughter away. Debbie said she'd stay with the older sister.

We hugged Debbie for a long time and said goodbye to her and the girl and drove away. They stood on the lawn in that late afternoon sun. Humidity like an inescapable memory. The next day my sister and I'd be in southern Alabama.

I've never been able to call Debbie and ask her if that baby—that little girl—is okay.

Filip Marinovich

HOUSEHOLDER SEEHORSE

                                      Seehorse has a vacation rug
        in her houseplanets dusting matters
here is Householder Seehorse
the sensational
            who measures closet space in her
                sleep with a tapemeasure
                      who returns me
to the right margin
when I float out too far
                feeds me the right margarine
so I don't get sent prematurely to a star

        The Death Star for instance might blow up my planet
        and if I'm on the Death Star
        will I be able to rescue the Earth in time

            After a walk is the best time to ice
            your left shoulder
                    the one the wave tore
            Your wing bone sticks out when you flex
            The codeine chicken goes PEEP PEEP
            it's not there
                what is there to ice
            there used to be an angel wing on that shoulder
            that's why that wing bone that sticks out when you flex
            is the one the chickens enjoy

                The peep hole I look through shows me
                the peepshow with swords
                      How knightly of you to notice this peepshow Lord
                      peepshow law will not go into effect until tomorrow
                      Act now and heist
                      the only diamond that cuts through illusion

The only Seehorse invented the guilliotine
Seehorse hung the guillotine from the mountain cliff
Seehorse and Rabbit went to
      Paris in 1919 to master the
           arts of the French Revolution,
               its foreign cuisine

      Dear Seehorse
      text me when you're free
      we can go rabbit dancing
      in the fox mouth for free
      what else is there to do in the recession please

Wake up in Sheep's Meadow Central Park
wolf salt burning a hole in which membrane
after the mountain top   outer space

      Rising into outer space
      that's why I can't sleep
      you say it's because I
      woke up in the middle of Central Park
      half nocturnal
      wolf salt burning a hole in which membrane
      after the mountain top   outer space

      the goat joker on the peak
               jester bells
                   on a green hat

      The peak is gone
      it was a jester hat spike all along

         No it wasn't
         Evidence is my skinned knees

Leave the door open when
you show the breeze in
guest of joker flesh

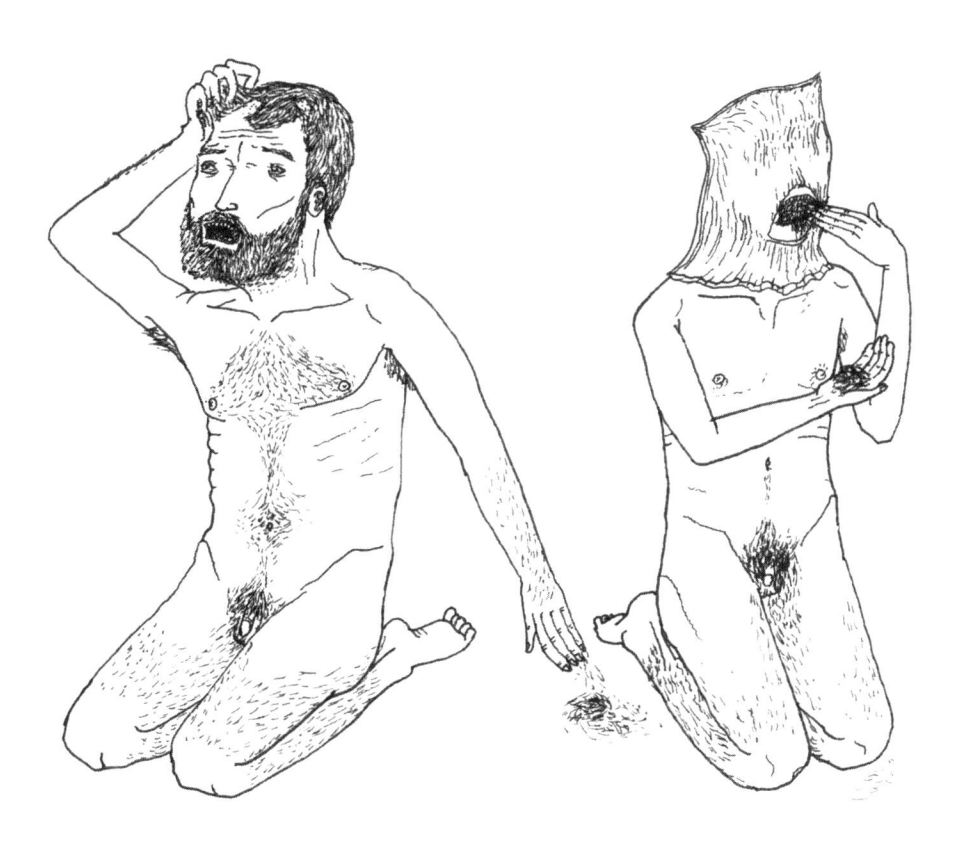

SAMUEL TOLZMANN UNTITLED

Samuel Tolzmann

PROCESS PIECE

In a *New York Times* review of the 2011 David Cronenberg film *A Dangerous Method*, A. O. Scott makes an important distinction when he remarks that modern psychoanalysis was a "way of understanding, and trying to assuage, some of the pain and intensity of being alive." Whether or not Scott intends to, he differentiates between this pain and that of *living*, by which I mean more material or pathological forms of suffering. His phrase has become useful to me as a way to pithily remind myself, and now my viewers as well, that *being alive* is always, to some degree, an inherently harrowing experience regardless of whether a person also registers the generally more self-evident but equally forceful pangs of *living*. I am a staunch believer in the notion that "the pain and intensity of being alive" is something that should be taken as seriously as circumstances will permit, and these drawings arose in large part from the need to artificially engender those circumstances.

In practice, this has meant an increased interest in the establishment of a certain set of conditions within a picture, rather than confessional depiction. My juvenilia, like that of many artists across every medium, was turbulent work treated as an opportunity to explain oneself. It's a cathartic tactic but in my personal experience it's often not a very interesting or successful one; it demanded little save a strong stomach. Now I use drawing and sculpture as ways to compose myself. I try to fold up the source personal narratives of the work inside comparatively unforthcoming images that turn viewers toward thematic concerns and away from, at least for a little while, their application to myself.

To do this I've learned to devise and employ cohesive and limited, yet flexible systems of related images; I spend a great deal of time planning individual drawings and groups of them before the pen touches the paper. My formal education is in literature and it's left me with an imagination inclined to narrative, reliant on symbol, and sensitive to the way the latter can sustain the former. From a variety of inspirations – e.g., the story of St. Agnes; monastic self-flagellation practices; Jean Cocteau movies; colonial-era American design, domestic tasks, and gender roles – I've fashioned a specific, minimal world that's odd without being excessively outlandish, a world of bedsheets and hirsute bodies that evokes my own painful preoccupations with monotheism and embodied masculine sexuality. To me, this visual vocabulary is object-correlative for my own experiences, but to the viewer it ideally gestures toward these issues while not divulging too much. The work involved in reading one's own material into and drawing the authorial material out of, these reticent and mysterious but obviously troubling images is meant to be the work of participating in an environment where the so-called selfish agonies are fully accepted and even taken with good humor. Some of the elements of these images are begged by my medium: in hair, for instance, I've located a versatile image that's suitably grounded in the everyday, is bound up in my own experience, and lends itself to fine pen-and-ink work (and embroidery, another medium of which I'm fond).

Once I've settled on content that accomplishes everything I need it to – a brainstorming process that causes gaps of months or even years between phases of work – the actual drawing is straightforward but laborious due to the level of detail and the fragility of the pen nibs used. Each of the drawings that appear here, 9x12 inches in the original, took between three weeks and three months to complete. During this period, I excised even more elements from the initial plan on-the-fly, further deepening and developing the complexity of those that remain. The duration and consideration of this process produces, I think, image systems that don't read as simple stand-ins for abstracts; they feel real and lived in. I hope the end results prove useful.

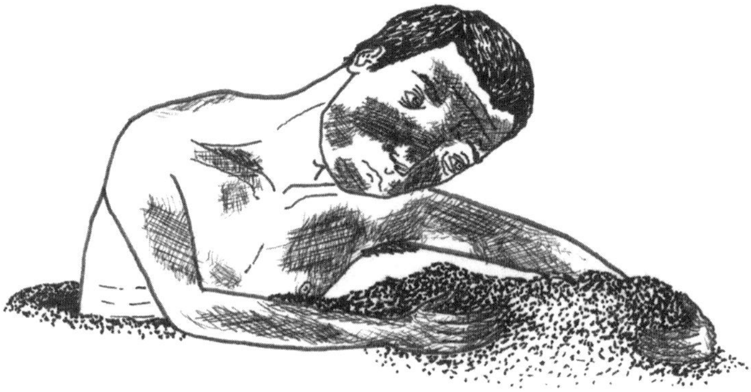

Laura Marie Marciano

after

is there a river that goes away?
will any of these people
continue to matter?
shoot me in the foot.
the beautiful baby
that you are creating
could have been
our baby.
i am going to be sad about you
for guess what
the rest of my life.

sparkle and shine

'what is the true price of an ICEE?'
I think on my way to the nook of your arm
on a Friday at 1pm.
i would like to bring back the aborted,
ask them if the glow of heaven is better.

Taylor Fox

NOT FOR PUBLIC DISPLAY

On his fortieth birthday, Mitchell killed a wolf. The Mexican gray had wandered into Georgie's Pinetop Pub. It had come there at night, confused like the lost snowbirds who pulled up from time to time in their Buicks or Lexus sedans, looking for directions back to the I-40.

This happened on a Wednesday. By Friday Georgie himself had hijacked the story, telling it with earnest, wide-eyed expressions as if it was lore from centuries ago. On fall Fridays the hunting guides began filing into the bar for a shot or two of Macallan's in preparation for their next group of restless suburbanites—mortgage brokers and building contractors mostly, their pockets bursting with surplus cash, looking for novel ways to spend it. Many of the suburbanites would handle their rifles with the trepidation of art museum curators gingerly toting Goya originals. The deeply etched lines on the guides' foreheads and above their mustaches would stay motionless, contemplating these hunting neophytes who awaited them in some blurry but quickly advancing future. The mustached men would then slam down one empty shot glass after another, until the sound blended into a single, martial rhythm.

"So there I was, washing and racking the short glasses—cuz Lincoln had by then downed about fifteen mud slides, so I was running out. Suddenly this beautiful, mangy wolf just comes walking through." Georgie had the TV behind him on full volume and was bellowing the story to the bar full of patrons.

"Again, Georgie. If you're gonna tell the story, get the details right. It was a Mexican gray wolf. And an animal can't be both beautiful and mangy." Jake shook his head and cracked a peanut shell, the remnants falling to the forest green cement floor.

Mitchell looked up at Georgie. He had sworn Georgie to secrecy—which, according to Georgie's interpretation, apparently permitted him to tell the story to customers. But Mitchell did not worry about these customers transporting the story back to the Valley—and, specifically, to his son. These men who sat circled around the bar didn't have much need for the horizon of new-build developments and low-hanging smog of the Valley.

Mitchell enjoyed the banter. He slipped unnoticed into the endless benevolent chatter of familiar voices around him—talking about him, joking with him, but never expecting or demanding an answer from him. His platoon in the Marines fifteen years earlier had let him quietly enjoy the same jocular communion between and among growing and grown men—22-year-old platoon sergeants bantering with 18-year-old privates and dragging Marlboros like they had smoked for centuries, their backs loaded with forty-pound canvas packs and the heavier, paternal burden of protector.

But tonight, Mitchell realized, Georgie's storytelling refused to let him stay hidden in the cloud of booming, drunken voices. Mitchell finished his beer, paid the tab, patted a still arguing Jake on the back, and left. It was a Friday night in the Arizona pinetop, and these men were thirsty, and they were angry for reasons they could not name. As the door behind Mitchell closed he could hear resume the cadence of shot glasses slamming down, one after another, atop the battlefield of a faded and chipped cherry wood bar.

The following Wednesday was Jack's first game of the season. After Mitchell finished his shift at Home Depot, he drove the seventy miles of windy two-lane highway that stepped, like a descending staircase, down to Phoenix.

When Mitchell arrived at the field the home team grandstands were half-filled, with large gaps of bare aluminum bleachers in the upper corners. He took a position toward the top of the bleachers beneath the press box. The second half had just begun. His son's team was down by three touchdowns. Mitchell wiped his glasses to try to peer through them and catch a glimpse of the lava-red "6" printed on Jack's black jersey amidst a flutter of spindly freshman legs and arms windmilling at the snap of the ball.

After the game Mitchell trudged in his splay-legged walk down across the rows of graying aluminum bleachers to the front railing. Beneath him the boisterous visiting team players trotted into the tunnel beneath the grandstand and back to their buses. Mitchell watched his son jog over to the chain-link fence and across the track on the far side of the field. A girl wearing a hooded zip-up sweatshirt leaned over the other side of the fence, bouncing on her tiptoes.

Jack looked like he was talking to her, although from the bleachers Mitchell only saw the long mane of hair poking from beneath his unblemished helmet. Mitchell watched the girl play with one of his son's shoulder pads, tucking it back beneath the green and black jersey. He watched Jack wave goodbye and start running across the field toward the bleachers, in search of his father.

"You like her." They sat on a steakhouse patio that abutted a carefully scooped man-made pond. Mallards drifted by as if on motorized tracks. It was early fall, and the colors had just started to turn in the pinetop. Mitchell wondered how ducks knew when to head south—whether the instinct crescendoed over days and weeks, until they could take it no longer and simply took flight in response to this urge mushrooming from within; or whether it was sudden, reflexive, inspirational.

Jack threw the mallard a piece of his bread. "Why do you think that?" Jack looked at him, keenly interested. This was Jack in irreducible form: never reacting with immediate joy or disappointment, but instead carefully feeling out his path, gathering more information before deciding whether to register as either "good" or "bad" the syllables being processed through the circuitry of his brain.

"Father's intuition. What's her name?"

"Ellie. We met in AP Physics. We're learning about the Higgs Boson." Jack grabbed another piece of bread and, his arm looping in the wide, miraculous arc of a rainbow, softly tossed it pondward. He then started looking around mechanically, his head turning sharply like a condor as he stared at his surroundings. "This species is peculiar. They sit at these circular pieces of wood covered with some kind of white fabric. And they wait for other members of their species to supply them with sustenance."

Mitchell dobbed the corners of this mouth with his napkin and managed to keep a straight face. Mitchell had invented this game for them to play when Jack was in second grade—when Mitchell had just started taking him on unsupervised visits to places that kids like, places like the go-kart track, or the arcade, or the cineplex—places with whirring noises and bright lights, enough to distract a third grader from the fact that his father was under psychiatric supervision and treatment for PTSD. On one of those early visits Jack had asked him about the pill he'd seen Mitchell pop into his mouth and wash down with a swig of Cherry Coke. Mitchell told him it was a vitamin for adults and Jack only nodded and turned toward the movie starting on the screen. Even at that young age he seemed to know when to direct his inquiries inward.

Finally Mitchell said, "You're right. And they exchange pieces of green paper with each other. Paper seems to be very important here."

Jack pointed at a couple holding each other's hands, canoodling at a candlelit booth toward the far corner. "Their physical contact appears to be neither for the purpose of mutual combat nor procreation. Is that this love of which this tribe speaks?"

Mitchell looked up and saw the couple for the first time. They looked to be in their mid-twenties. The man wore a beige and black plaid fedora, a navy blue pinstriped sport coat, and a button-down shirt tucked into his corduroys. The woman wore a blue camisole and dark jeans. A carafe of red wine stood in the center of the table, next to the brass candleholder and its enclosed, unwavering flame.

Mitchell watched the couple for a moment. Throughout his childhood the precocious little scientist had posed to his parents a dizzying array of questions. In preschool, after Jack and his classmates had been asked to draw a picture of the planet Earth, Jack had returned home and asked his parents why penguins living on the South Pole weren't always hanging upside down. The following year he had asked why smaller scorpions were more venomous than the larger ones. In first grade he asked how DVD technology worked. But Mitchell couldn't recall Jack ever asking him for a definition of love. Mulling over an answer to give to that unasked question, Mitchell had none. Mitchell was more versed in death than in love. Death, in all its forms: quick, combustible death, flitting like a prairie mouse; painful, extended death, long enough to hold up for display the crumbling of the soul itself; death of best friends, death of enemy soldiers, righteous death, senseless death, death from afar, death up close, all within what felt like the grimy sandswept footprint of the Creator. Death of kindness. Death of hope. On those preternaturally quiet desert nights while he and his convoy lurched like an armored centipede across the disconsolate land, Mitchell had learned only this about love: that it explained man's fear of death.

But Mitchell did not yet wish to speak to his son about death.

"Did you hear me?" Jack was talking again.

"No. Please repeat."

"I asked you"—nodding at the young couple—"is that an example of this love of which this species speaks?"

Mitchell swigged lustily from his water glass. Then he plunked down two rumpled twenty-dollar bills on the table and rose to leave. "I do not know, son. We need to keep watching."

"The end of days is this Saturday, you know." Jack said this as he sat on the patio railing of their first story motel room.

"Where'd you hear that?" Mitchell yelled from the motel bathroom as he flushed.

"I read it on a blog. Some preacher in the Catskills whose been stockpiling food and water for ten years. Okay! I got it. Check it out." Jack swung down from his perch on the patio railing and walked back into the motel room. "If you had to be punished in Hell for all eternity, what punishment would you rather have: to have to re-live your worst moments in life over and over, like it was on repeat; or, to have to run around the world, again and again, without ever stopping?"

Mitchell walked back into the room and sprawled across one of the double beds. The muted television displayed a sincere-looking man with a graying comic book hero coif, wearing a camel-colored suit and tenderly holding a cylindrical, chrome-shaped object that looked like a curling iron. His lips seemed to blur with their rapid shuttle movements up and down. An eight hundred number was emblazoned in the upper left hand corner of the screen.

"I'd take the running."

"Why?"

"I'm a good runner."

"No you're not. You don't run. You drink beer."

Mitchell sat up, scratching his temple with an index finger. "Because it would be a good distraction."

"Distraction from what?"

"From those worst moments of your life. The ones you can't ever put out of your mind."

Jack stood looking at a Seurat print on the wall, his back to Mitchell. Suddenly he turned around and looked directly at his father. Mitchell watched his son lick his lips thoughtfully. He could almost see his son's unspoken questions billow and twist upward, like steam from a glacial thawing. He waited.

But Jack asked no questions. "I can accept that," his son finally said.

"So then what's your idea of Heaven?" Mitchell exhaled, slumping down into the bed but still studying his son—big for his age, likely full-grown, the pigeon-toed stance inherited from Mitchell, but the long, nimble fingers belonging to Jack's mother, a guitarist's fingers. But there was, in the center of his son, an untraceable otherness that came from neither one of his parents. The God particle, Mitchell thought, recalling a phrase he had heard somewhere.

"I don't know." Jack looked at himself in the dresser mirror, pulling up one shirt sleeve and examining a stringy bicep that he playfully flexed up and down. "I just picture a lot of white. Like the place you went to for a while when I was a kid."

Mitchell froze. "What do you remember?"

"Well. Charlene was the name of the lady at the desk. And she always gave me Jolly Ranchers from a fish bowl. And she smiled a lot, and had really yellow teeth. And I remember hating when she smiled." Jack kicked the bed frame gently. "I spent most of the time there with her while Mom went into your room. Right?"

Mitchell sat up, scratching the shade of stubble across his chin. "If you say so." He winked, then got up. "I promise you Heaven is a lot better than that place." He grabbed his car keys and flipped them to his son. "Let's go for a drive. You're driving."

"I haven't passed my road test yet. What if I get in a wreck? I'm not even insured. Wouldn't your insurance go way up?"

"You're not going to crash." Mitchell grabbed his jacket from the writing desk across from the foot of the bed.

"Where are we going?"

"Wherever you take us."

Jack drove them up the Beeline Highway. Past the scrub brush and the fiercely blinking lights of the casino. Past the reservation land and toward national forest acreage, as they drove along the road back to Mitchell's cabin.

"We'll get halfway there. Then you turn back. Okay?" Mitchell said, looking down at Jack's feet to make sure he was using only his right foot on the pedals.

They passed the criss-crossing strands of barrel cacti, past the faraway mesa reddening under the sinking sun. They wound their way past the desert foothills, their crowns yellowed and bare, like a crowd of old bowed heads. They sped past the disordered columns of standing sahuaro, their arms raised in eternal surrender.

After a little while Mitchell told Jack to head back to the Valley. He slowed the car along the dirt shoulder, waiting for traffic behind him to pass. When no cars were behind him he made a U-turn, driving right in front of a pot-bellied Navajo merchant and his roadside stand. The Navajo's gray hair was tied in a pony-tail. Under the blue tarp of his stand stood two card tables, across which were laid jewelry and framed prints. He looked up hopefully at Mitchell and Jack.

"He thinks we're going to stop. I feel bad. I think we should buy something."

They got out of the car and made their way to the white rectangular table with an array of beads, jewelry, small painting prints in shabby wooden frames, faded price stickers hanging loosely off each. Beyond the looming ring of desert foothills, their crowns ringed with clumps of sallow desert scrub, a deep pink horizon boiled like the surface of a bubbling cauldron. Mitchell watched his son slide-step slowly around the table as he browsed. Jack had done that side-stepping shuffle since he was three years old—feet moving, but eyes fixed on whatever held his attention in that moment. Their SeaWorld trip had been the genesis of the side-step shuffle. For Jack the entire world was one sprawling aquarium to which he pressed his face to the glass. As he stood near his son, watching him peer at a hawk-shaped bronze brooch, Mitchell himself felt like glass; a glass lantern enclosing the bright flame that thawed the world.

Seaworld. That was back when Mitchell—and all of the biochemical packaging that comprised him—could feel right side up without meds; back when his thoughts did not derail him and Molly was happy and smiled whenever he looked at her. They'd had plans to see a new place in a different state every year. Then he went to the hospital for those years—months initially, broken up like iceberg fragments whenever he would return home for a brief stay, but in the end amounting to a passage of years.

Mitchell walked over to another table, this one smaller, where two boys of about the same age, somewhere around ten years old, sat. One wore a Phoenix Suns jersey and had a dark curtain of hair that fell halfway down his back. The other wore an oversized flannel shirt, shorts, and basketball sneakers. They were both staring intently at a smartphone that the ponytailed boy held. One of them looked up at Mitchell, then back down at the phone he held. Then he looked up at Mitchell again, and back to the phone. He elbowed his friend in the ribcage.

"What?" Flannel Shirt said. He followed Ponytail's gaze all the way over and up to Mitchell.

"Are you sure? Can you make it bigger?" Flannel Shirt asked.

"Dude. It's him."

"Awesome!"

By now Jack walked over to Mitchell. "What's going on?"

"Don't know."

"You mind if I see that?" Jack extended one hand. Ponytail handed over his black phone in its white rubber case, the padding smudged with use. Jack pushed one thumb a few times on the screen, transfixed at what he was watching.

"Well? What is it?"

Mitchell watched the "o"-shape of Jack's lips enlarge until finally he looked up at his father. "It's you."

In the three days that followed, Mitchell rode the sharp upward ascent of Internet fame that accompanies "going viral". His crash course began on the ride back to the hotel with his son—who, speaking in a hurried fashion, explained the nuances of YouTube. Prior to that conversation, the word "YouTube" had been a part of the argot of the younger generation that Mitchell occasionally tossed into conversations with his son more for shock value, to remind him that he still kept a parental vigil over the new technology hoarding the attention of Jack and his friends. In reality, though, Mitchell had known very little about YouTube.

But now his son explained how many people had achieved fame and riches through the "everyman" access to this website: aspiring actors, singers, rappers, ranters spewing anti-government vitriol in five to ten-minute segments, amateur comedians trying to make a faceless audience laugh, evangelists condemning gay marriage in unedited sermons, inventors advertising their hydrogen-fueled rocket cars. Jack also explained to him the importance of "hits", which was (from the viewpoint of the website): the more, the better.

In one week the video clip of Mitchell and the wolf had gathered over half a million hits.

After Mitchell had dropped Jack off at school the next morning he made a beeline the eighty miles back to town and went straight to Georgie's for answers. According to George, one of the cooks—who was also a bassist in a local death metal band called Three Buck Chuck—had found the video surveillance footage of "the mano-to-mano", as they called it. In an effort to promote Three Buck Chuck's demos, the cook/bassist looped them into the surveillance video clip before posting it on YouTube, so that the chaotic sound of Three Buck Chuck served as the soundtrack while viewers watched man face off wolf. But no one, including the cook/bassist, anticipated how popular the thing would become.

George swore to Mitchell that he had never even told the cook/bassist that the bar had surveillance cameras—or that the equipment itself was kept on one of Georgie's office shelves, buried behind a row of signed baseballs and football jerseys. But the cook/bassist had known, and after "the mano-to-mano," he apparently decided that *this* was *the* video-recorded lightning in a bottle that Three Buck Chuck needed to promote itself. For his transgressions and disloyalty Georgie fired the cook/bassist, but not before the clip had been uploaded onto YouTube.

"I'm sorry, Mitch. I let you down." Georgie rubbed his scruffy salt-and-pepper jowls.

"It's not your fault."

"And if Jack was my kid, I would've told him about it already anyways. It's an act of heroism, is what it is. Your kid's probably proud more than anything else. Why keep that a secret?"

"I just would've preferred to, is all."

"Did I tell you I fired the cook?"

By Friday Mitchell started receiving calls on his cell phone. One was from a blonde-coiffed local TV news personality named Bradley Ballard. With other bar patrons surreptitiously inching closer to eavesdrop, Mitchell's polite rejections for one-on-one interviews were done in a low muffle, into the crook of his arm, straining the cord of the phone from the wall over the beer taps from which the phone hung. Mr. Ballard, though, brought more to Mitchell's attention than just an interview request.

"I said, what do you think about the whole ARGO-Nauts thing?" Ballard repeated his question.

Mitchell had heard of the group. "ARGO"—"Animal Rights Group Omnipresent"—was an animal rights group that had gained some notoriety at Yosemite for staging a sit-in with actual wildlife—including bears (under the supervision of bear trainers, at least one of whom had bear mace and a tranquilizer gun at the ready)—as part of their protest group. The event had escaped any serious maulings from its fellow wildlife protesters; its bold efforts had won it a wave of popularity on the west coast.

"I don't know anything about that," Mitchell said, and hung up the phone.

By the end of the week he did. ARGO-Nauts had found out where he worked and set up protest stations outside of the Home Depot entrance. The first week was manageable; the protest force numbered less than five kids from the junior college two miles down Route 87, and because the YouTube video was a bit grainy they did not know the face of the person who they were protesting. Standing near the propane tank racks outside, relentlessly tweeting updates to their Twitter feeds, they looked more like loiterers than protesters.

The second week the college kids had gotten organized: v-necked black t-shirts with "ARGO-NAUTS" stenciled across the front in white lettering. Someone had brought a blue and red U of A Wildcats canopy cross it and had set it up next to the winter rye grass display by lawn and garden annex. Someone else had brought a camping stove, turkey burgers and buns, and coolers filled with Vitamin Water. They sat and ate and occasionally shouted phrases in unison—making them look less like loiterers than tailgaters. That week a few of the customers Mitchell helped would crack jokes about walking back to their pick-ups, removing their Remington 700 rifle from their gun racks, and taking target practice at the protesters' bottles of designer water. Mitchell would purse his lips in an indecipherable look—either one of agreement or reproach—and would simply continue helping them find a certain size steel hex bolt, or the aisle where the multimeters hung, or a soldering kit.

But by Halloween weekend the furtive jokes had turned into hostile stares, mutterings, and—finally—a shoving match between a retired bus driver and the ARGO-NAUT protest leader, a short, muscled young man with curved sideburns like fish hooks. The number of protesters by then numbered well over twenty. Protesters paced around outside with life-size signs depicting the dead, poached carcasses of Mexican gray wolves. More pushing and shoving. Police were called. They came, took down complaints, left.

That Thursday Mitchell's boss Gary walked him down the timber aisle, planks of wood stacked twenty feet high on either side.

"Look, I know that none of this is your fault, that you did what you had to do with that mountain lion," he said, wiping a strand of hair across his beaded, lined forehead. Gary had the perpetually anxious manner of a spy fleeing assassins. "But this isn't doing anything for business. Customers are getting annoyed. Yesterday we almost had an incident."

"Incident?"

"Involving one of the protesters and a customer. And a drop saw. My point is, management has to do what it has to do." Gary paused. "Just like you did."

When the newly unemployed Mitchell walked out a few minutes later, a handful of protesters loitered near a display of propane tanks and energy efficient window panes. Their signs were propped up against a soda machine. Two of them were rapturously texting. One young man dressed in cargo shorts, a tank top and a safari hat, watched every person coming and going. "Who are we looking for again?" Mitchell overhead him asking the other texter. "I think that was him," Mitchell heard Safari say several seconds later. But by then Mitchell was at the door of his car, where he had sunk into the tattered vinyl driver's seat and headed home.

The next night was darts night at Georgie's. Mitchell sat at a table with Jake, a half-full pitcher of beer between them. Mitchell watched Georgie sail a dart over the board, embedding itself in the wall. As Mitchell rose to take his turn, Jake nudged him, nodding toward the TV in the corner of the game room.

"It's not surprising at all that this happened. He has demonstrated violent tendencies, dating back to his time in the military. And I'm talking above and beyond the call of duty. Let's just say this isn't the first living being that he's killed. He even spent time in a mental institution. But then they release him—back into the wild, so to speak—and *this* happens." Channel 7 was interviewing an ARGO-Naut whose name, Edward Hauser, was emblazoned at the bottom of the screen.

The TV now had Georgie's attention. "Hey Rick, turn it off," he said to one of the bouncers manning the rear entrance.

"No. Keep it on." Mitchell was out of his chair now, his eyes never wavering from the battered projection tube set. Edward Hauser went on: "The fact remains that this particular individual is a veteran of the Iraq War. And, my sources have all confirmed that he had an extended stay in a mental health facility for PTSD. He had a history of domestic violence involving his wife and son. But the ARGO-Nauts aren't here to sound the anti-war trumpet. I want to talk about us, about our mission, about a quickly vanishing species that has now become just more entertainment fodder, nothing more than something for somebody to kill time over their lunch break surfing the Net." Edward paused, winded.

While Edward spoke, neither Georgie nor Jake snuck a glance toward Mitchell. If either one had he would have seen that Mitchell was no longer standing there. He might have noticed Mitchell walking—calm, unhurried, placing a twenty on the bar for two draft beers and a half-eaten tray of appetizers picked from the happy hour menu—out the front entrance and to his car.

As Mitchell left Georgie's and pulled onto the roadway, his thoughts were only on his immediate surroundings: on the handful of pick-ups and Jeeps parked at odd angles on the small dirt strip that passed for Georgie's parking lot; on the DVD rental store across the way where he and a pregnant Molly would go rent horror movies, laughing about how their child would come out of the womb already desensitized to violence. He thought of the smooth feel of the newly paved asphalt road beneath the tires, like riding a gust of wind across a glassine lake surface.

The wolf had walked into the bar through the back door that Georgie had forgotten to close. Even in those winter months Georgie usually left it open because of the stifling heat produced by the bar's wood paneling, poor ventilation, and dozens of hunters standing mashed together, sweating beneath flannel garments. It was a Wednesday, a few minutes short of midnight. The somnolent movements of two patrons bookended the bar: one man in a fleece jacket playing video poker, a duffle bag at the foot of his stool; and an ancient-looking woman with gray wisps of hair seeping through her blond dye job, gazing vacuously up at the TV above the bar as she tapped her cigarette against an ashtray.

It was a male. He was no bigger than a golden lab retriever. Matted rust-colored fur ran the length of his back. Flecks of brown and black coloring spattered his ribs and flank. Bare patches along his underbelly revealed pink skin dotted with sores. The twin parabolas of his ears were jagged on the tips. One ear had a numbered blue tag on it. His white paws and muzzle remained pristine.

Mitchell had just downed his free birthday shot of Crown Royal and was rolling the shot glass between his thumb and forefinger. His eyes flitted back and forth between the TV and the empty glass. When he saw the wolf he looked over at the other occupants of the bar, expecting yells and shrieks to come from them. But they sat fixated on a reality dating show on the TV. Georgie continued cleaning tumblers with a soaked rag, his back to Mitchell and the wolf.

The wolf did not seem anxious. Instead it looked up at the framed hunting photos of hunters and their kills—moose, twelve-point bull elk, a brown bear—with the mild curiosity of a tourist strolling past exhibits at the zoo. Mitchell suddenly recalled overnight camping trips in the heart of the Coconino Forest, curled up in his sleeping bag, one arm slung over a six-year-old Jack. He would tell his son to listen hard for wolves, although Mitchell had trekked those areas enough to know that the wolves had fled long ago, that the wails his son heard at night were nothing more than coyotes of the type that would pop up from time to time even back in the Valley, skulking around at dusk in sleepy new developments, looking for wandering calicos and Yorkies. Mitchell had heard of a wildlife foundation re-introducing a small group of Mexican grays back in eastern Arizona, up by Blue Ridge. If this one was from that group, he had traveled over sixty miles to arrive, unceremoniously, at Georgie's Pinetop Pub.

The wolf swung its head around and looked squarely at Mitchell. In his eyes—murky like brackish water, unrevealed even in the flickering light of the TV and the neon Captain Morgan sign on the wall—Mitchell caught the opaque shimmer of madness. The wolf was old, hungry, but madness had made him forget of such matters. Still watching Mitchell, the wolf started to pant half-heartedly, his tongue unfurling until it hung just over his bottom fangs. Then it stopped panting, his muzzle closing and his head cocked toward the wall as if someone on the other side was whispering to him.

The TV rambled on. The clinking sound of tumblers being placed on the drying rack continued. The mad wolf and the war vet stared at one another.

Georgie put the last tumbler on the drying rack. He turned around and looked at the wolf.

"What's that," he said.

The wolf sprung toward Georgie, scrambling onto an empty bar stool. Remembering the tackling drills from two-a-day practices in high school—"head up, wrap up"—Mitchell lowered one shoulder into the wolf's side. He could feel the wolf's ribcage bend on impact, could hear the wolf's surprised exhalation. The soused woman at the bar was now rousing from her stupor, chanting "Oh-my-God-oh-my-God-oh-my-God". From the corner of his eye Mitchell saw Georgie running to the far side of the bar and reaching for his sawed-off shotgun strapped beneath the bottom of the ice chest. The wolf bounced off of Mitchell, who grabbed the empty bar stool and took one long stride to where the wolf was scrambling to stand up on the cement floor. Mitchell stood between the wolf and Georgie so that he wouldn't be able to get a clear shot. Mitchell held the bar stool out in front of him.

The wolf leaped again, this time at Mitchell, who could hear the woman's chanting dissolve into garbled shrieks and prayers. Mitchell angled one stool leg toward the wolf's open maw. The wolf clamped down, and Mitchell could feel the wood start to cave beneath the force. Mitchell staggered backward until both he and the wolf fell. The animal's jaw remained resolutely fastened to the stool leg.

Mitchell straddled the wolf's kicking hind legs and with all of his strength, pressed one forearm against his windpipe. Through the thicket of fur Mitchell could feel the wolf's frantic heartbeat. Mitchell's face was now inches from his. The animal's breath smelled like the fields of rotting seaweed Mitchell used to find washed ashore near his grandparents' beach cottage when he was a child. He pushed harder until he felt the wolf's chest shuddering in its efforts to suck in breath. With his jaw partially open and locked onto the stool leg wedged between it, the wolf looked like he was smiling.

Mitchell pressed down harder. The wolf bit down harder.

Mitchell saw the wood giving way beneath the wolf's teeth. He could feel a lump of cartilage trying to bob up and down, delving deep for breath. The wolf's eyes now the rust color of his back, as if the hue had bled from there and seeped into his stare. And something else pooled there: some vague awareness, or understanding, like a sleeping train passenger awakening and suddenly remembering he was surrounded by others.

Mitchell could hear the drunk woman's continued screams. Georgie was yelling at him to get out of the way; Mitchell shook his head no. He pressed his forearm harder until the tip of his elbow pinned into place that node of cartilage in the wolf's windpipe. Mitchell swallowed, even as the wolf could not. He pressed down on the wolf's throat until twin droplets of tears escaped, dissolving into the fur of the wolf's white muzzle. Keeping his jaws clenched on the nearly severed wooden stool leg, the Mexican gray cast a last sideways glance at Mitchell, and died that way.

Mitchell passed the two-story brick elementary school. A few minutes later the dingy glass-and-steel credit union and the Indian restaurant passed by. Finally, sitting with a silver radar dish perched atop it like a woman's tilted sunbonnet, was KYAK, the local television station. As he pulled into the parking lot a sliver of sunlight leaked over the pine treeline behind the mint green wood-slatted building.

The beauty of a small town is: Everything is a five-minute drive from everything else.

Mr. Hauser's pontifications ended at about the eighteen-minute mark of his scheduled thirty-minute interview. As Jake reached for a lime by the beer taps he finally noticed that Mitchell was no longer in the bar. He then turned in the direction of Georgie's gasp and saw that his father was instead there, on the TV. He was there, walking into the frame of the camera. He was there, taking one calm stride toward Mr. Hauser. He was there, one open hand raised back. And then that open hand was there, striking Mr. Hauser's cadaverous cheek. The interviewer looked on, his face a misplaced mask of mild discomfort, like he was watching a Mardi Gras float rolling through a funeral procession.

The blow to Mr. Hauser's face stung the air. It sounded like a slate tile dropped on a classroom desk. Then they heard the sounds of scuffling shoes and A/V equipment banging off camera.

And then Mitchell was gone, one additional calm stride across the frame and into pixilated oblivion.

"Oh, boy," said Georgie.

"He really did it now, huh," said Jake.

This, too, ended up on YouTube.

Georgie offered to call the park ranger to pick up the wolf's body. But Mitchell was already wrapping the wolf in a blue tarp he had in the bed of his pick-up. Before he left, he had Georgie promise not to tell anyone what Mitchell had done.

He drove past the Blue Ridge campgrounds and down a rutted dirt road that hooked around the more densely wooded side of the lake, the side where no one camped. He drove until the road ended in a mass of tangled bramble. He carried the shovel and the tarp-rolled dead wolf in his arms. He passed through the thick congregation of pinyon pine and up along a corridor of sumac leading to an outcropping overlooking a water reservoir below. This was the place where Mitchell had taken his son camping years ago; the place where he had assured him that there were no wolves, that he was safe beneath his sleeping bag.

He looked down at the blue tag on the wolf's ear. He noted the tag number so he could tell the wolf preserve from which the Mexican gray had presumably wandered. He looked up at the monstrous ponderosa pines all around him. He walked around the trees until he found it: the words "King Kong" etched out ten years earlier by his five-year-old son. Jack had chosen the name because the tree dwarfed the others around it. Mitchell had cupped his hands over his son's; he guided Jack's hands with his own as Jack carved each letter into the bark. "What next?" Jack asked him after finishing each letter, and Mitchell would tell him the next one to carve. Jack also asked if the carving was hurting the tree, and Mitchell assured his son that it wasn't. But Mitchell hadn't really known, then or now.

The soil was still damp from a light shower the night before. Mitchell laid the wolf down in the shade of King Kong. Softly, slowly, he ran one sun-stained hand the length of the wolf's russet fur. A breeze whispered over the wolf's still body, raising a few tufts of fur as if they were rising to the touch of Mitchell's hand. He picked up the shovel and dug, careful not to scatter any dirt on top of the wolf yet. A vulture landed high on a ponderosa branch above them, creeping further out onto the branch, closer to this burial. Mitchell waved and shouted a few expletives, but it did not flinch. He then hurled the shovel, javelin-style, straight up toward the branch. It hit a spot on the tree several feet short of the vulture, who unfolded its wings, white feathers outlined against indigo, and departed with a casual flapping as the shovel clattered to the ground a few yards from Mitchell.

    He stood there a moment, panting from the yelling and the javelin throw. When he caught his breath, he started to dig again, in this sacred place. This place where he would someday take his son, by then an adult, and tell him about all of those things. Things that Mitchell had seen. Things he had done, while strapped to a helmet and a machine gun. He would tell him about ending a man's life as if you were hanging up the phone. He would tell his son what he had learned about the soul of man: that if it was stretched and squeezed out of its original dimensions, it would spend the rest of its years trying to crawl, inch by inch, back to its first form. Mitchell dug for a long time in that place, where secrets were not yet endangered but instead blithely grazed, waiting for extinction.

Cean Gamalinda

recut for b

all my passwords are either vanilla or jesus / can we go to Popeyes is it open? / I want some biscuits / I want some biscuits / let's get biscuits / let's listen to Watch the Throne / no this is dubstep / no this is trance / no this is triphop / no this is Skrillex / where is George / why isn't George coming / I'm not gonna juice with him ever again / we're not gonna juice with him again / call George, let's juice / this is Elliot Smith / this is the dubstep remix of Elliot Smith / this is Skrillex Smith / this is slave mentality / this is divine ordinance / this is a city ordinance / you can't park there / move your car I'm parked in front of you / I love you, no, really, i love you / I am the echoes of the Orphic harp / no you're thinking Morpheus / no that's the Matrix / oh my god / I love Keanu too / you are Eurydice's heartbeat / oh wait she's dead / this is a solution without a problem / this is the Final Solution / this is the Final Countdown / this is the blitzkrieg / are you awake? / this is the zeitgeist / this is my uncle's 40th birthday party / this is my inaugural address / hey wake the fuck up / hey internalize this / this is Reaganomics without the rich / hey I'm Ronald Reagan / hey I'm Ronald Reagan / I need another 40 / hey I'm Ronald Reagan / do you have any change? / can you trickle me some cash for a 40? / can you tickle me? / what? / what? / no I didn't say anything / what? / what? / what? / what? / haha ohmygod I know / "If music be the food of love, play on" / do you like Whitman? / Whitman wrote that / ok that's bullshit / that was Shakespeare / that was shaky / I am shaking / i think i love you / let me burrow into you like a tick / let me into your skin / let me steep myself in your flesh / i know this is weird / i know this is awkward / i know this is awkward / I used to know a guy but he's dead now / honestly i thought i loved you / but like who the fuck even are you / let's go to Red Lobster / everyone loves Red Lobster / you would like Red Lobster and we wouldn't even have to give you an identity to go there / it's great / it's great / they have these giant fake lobsters over the front entrance / a giant steel lobster / a giant copper lobster / a giant wireframe copper lobster / you can touch it / it's great / it's got these giant claws / I love claws / "I should have been a pair of

Red Lobster claws / scuttling across the floors of silent seas" / you know, Prufrock / you know, Eliot / yes, Elliott Smith / yes, T.S. Elliott Smith the lovelorn Modernist / no, I doubt they'll play any Elliott Smith at Red Lobster / WHAT THE FUCK DO YOU MEAN THEY WON'T PLAY ELLIOTT SMITH / I NEED THAT SWEET RELEASE / WILL THEY STILL PLAY SKRILLEX / DO THEY SERVE JUICE THERE / well then FUCK THAT / CALL GEORGE / FUCK GEORGE / FUCK JUICE I DON'T WANT ANY / LET'S GET DRINKS / LET'S GET COORS / LET'S GET BUDWEISER / LET'S GET HEINEKEN / "HEINEKEN? FUCK THAT SHIT! / PABST / BLUE / RIBBON!" / listen: Tanzanian pea-berry medium roast at the Trader Joe's / double ginger peach mocha twist sangria bubble squeeze in the rain at Argo Tea / orange white grape pink grapefruit white tea at the New Wave Cafe / wow that was really dense / Let's break it down / Let's unpack that / Let's Stay Together by Al Green / I NEED A 40 / i think you should stop drinking / so do i / I NEED A 40 / look / if i speak critically in any capacity, i mean only that i am every sadness that i explicate / if i sing of arms and a man, then those are my arms and i am that man / if the birds done broke loose in the sky then so have i / yeah / i guess you could say i hate poems with form / "Fuck you. / Everything has form. / You have form you asshole. / You have form you fucking asshole" / yeah, i guess you could say i'm obsessed with irrigation in third-world countries / shouts out to people with two first names / i'm lookin at you Jason Alexander / i'm lookin at you Rick Ross / yeah you wish, Jerry Lee Lewis / omg / "I got the results of the test back—I definitely have breast cancer" / blame it on the gangster rap / the elephant is pearl aloof / bro / tell me why my mother died this morning in Iowa City / i know this is weird / i know this is awkward / but do you wear underwear under your tights? / the sometime knowledge of dreams / To dream to die / to die, perchance to sleep / i work for the biggest educational company in the business / Et tu, Booty? / "send down one bay shrimp salad sandwich" / AC/DC was Australian? / paradigm shift / Ask and you shall receive! (sexy voice) / this is stupid / this is so stupid / god this is so stupid / Shakira / has fallen / we love you / get up / i am afraid i will never meet someone because i never meet anyone / goddam / my crippling retrospective anxiety over social interactions other people immediately forget / they won't remember me / then what remains? / then who is left? / then this must be the face of death / then this must be the guy who agreed to run across the street to the liquor store / no beer no party / always be drunk on something am i right! / isn't that Baudelaire? / i think you mean Booty-laire / i think you mean Bau-de-lai-re / i think i mean Booty-laire / fuck a rose / a name is a joke people tell you is funny / "Oct. 2, i hired a frankfurter wagon to give away free "wieners" / This was a pun on my name / Anything or anybody can have anything or anybody's name" / David Brazil / Anthony Madrid / Hannah Montana / know me, then, as Destiny's Child / c'mon you can get funkier than that / i love the alphabet / abcdefghijklmnopqrstuvwxyz / emuyhsnfbxralidwtzvqpgkcjo / awblpgjxymouqtdnkciehrzfvs / nlszbdqjmyawufcgeitorkhpxv / ipgjrnxuyedfzomcqthbwlkvas / abcdefghiu—/ WAIT / I DID IT / I'VE DONE IT / I'VE PUT U AND I TOGETHER IN THE ALPHABET / SO THIS IS THE POWER OF POETRY / who's got winner on this game? / i'm playing next game / i call next game / brah / watch me on the news i'm runnin game / let's go outside / it's cold outside / it's ok i'm wearing a vodka tonic / i / am on my knees / and i'm wearing toe rings / Amsterdam: she called me and i said / in college i am dead / "breathless horror" / erotic displacement / redundant rhyme / name-dropping drugs as a masturbatory gesture / but don't you know it all comes down to juxtaposition in the] end? / obsessive alienation / Dave Matthews Band / sutured longing in memories of soft tweed blankets on the lawn of the Riviera, last summer with Dave Matthews Band / "sometimes my arms bend back" / my body electric needs an outlet / i will die / CORRECTION: i will die alone / dead bird in a dead oak tree / and i don't know it's probably Modern from where you're standing / yo DJ! / put on some Angelo Badalamenti / all faces becoming the same speaking convex glass / "it was all a dream / i used to read Word Up Magazine" but now they tell me print is dead / i measure out my life in tablespoons of you / biting wind! / unfamiliar air! / Tom bought a kazoo and / guys / Tom / guys / Tom bought a kazoo and he knows all of Bohemian Rhapsody / what happens to meaning when civilization dies? / oh get over yourself / "do you guys know what noir is?" / yeah, black / it is / so easy / to kill a fly / it is / one of the most easy things to do / Spoiler Alert: Bob Marley is dead / sorry man, i'm just on way too much peyote right now / cut me with the uncut hair of graves / drop me inyour deep foundries / melt me Terminator 2-style / Corona beach-baked lobster at Red Lobster / have we talked about this before? / I see you hiding on the floor behind the couch! / Mothers and Fathers, I see you all and weeping turn to yell Give it up! / I was a track star for Mineola Prep / and how about this: we call it The Renaissance / GEORGE I / forgot / you know what they say / you either got it or you don't / and i might / but who do you think you are? / no really who are you / i thought i knew but already i've forgotten / "Guillaume Apollinaire is dead" / and i don't think she ever called him back / "Because the wind is high, it blows my mind" / does it smell like pot to you? / i know i've been sweating but doesn't it smell like pot to you? / "you look ravishing this evening" / you are all the different names for breasts / you are all the unflushed toilets in the city of Chicago tonight / you walk into the room and the temperature is raised three degrees / celsius / you, "light of my life, fire of my loins. My sin, my soul," are the seagull chewing on a half-finished Big Mac in the Jewel-Osco parking lot / you are the coke bust on the evening news / you are misery in the form of something beautiful, charming in the way flowers on a grave are charming / you are banality with clothes on / you are sentiments smushed together and set before me / you're my Rushmore / you are a rush of blood to the head by Coldplay / you are the band Coldplay / you are Coldplay / you are your roommate's DVD copy of Failure to Launch starring Matthew Mcconaughey and Sarah Jessica Parker in her third feature film since the finale of Sex and the City / you are the Fountain of Latona / you are the walls of Jericho / you are Francois Truffaut / Surely you are the movie Airplane / you are why the caged bird sings / you are the symmetry of the sky upon the sea / you are the life story of every person I've ever sat next to on a train / you are a pregnant woman smoking cigarettes for shock value / you are the moment when setting yourself on fire becomes passe / you are the mist on the windshield when Scully sighs past Mulder's lips / you, sweet sunset of my soul, are six, no, five and a half jars of nutella on my kitchen counter / "I wanna get lost in your rock n roll and drift away" / you the dog's dried salivations on the morning paper / you unending rain / you collapsing glacier / you the fire that melts to make whole / "you got a face with a view" / you the older Chinese woman at the Bryn Mawr Starbucks every night calling me a pretty boy and asking if i want her sweets / you the guy who walks into the bookstore, sees there's a poetry reading, then walks back out / you the homeless man dropping his vodka on the train / you the potential lover asking just exactly how old i am / you the potential lover adjusting your methods of interaction based on just exactly how old i am / you the scholar in the armchair / you the scholar on the couch in the bar adjacent to the movie theater / you the voice of art / you the fart in the crowded elevator / you interrogation of our cultural lexicon / you bent along the curved embankment of the Chicago Riverwalk / your hair browned from last summer's sun / is this you or a memory that haunts me? / you Rube Goldberg heart / you squashpics.com / you Antietam foot massage / you are the Red that matadors hold up to inflame such passions in the bull that it loses itself / and i like to imagine that the way i lose myself in you is tragic to some comparable proportion / *AHEM* "in this life, to die is not new / but to live, of course, is no newer"/ TURN MY MIC UP / TURN UP MY MIC / Versace Parataxis / listen: imitation is not always a matter of personal conviction / listen: imitation does not preclude generativity / listen: the man on the bus said poetry's dead / please tell me how i can turn this two-liter of pineapple Faygo into a bong / Sweet Thames, run softly till I end my song / I'd rather be dead than listening to Tool / O! Saturnalia! / sweet secondhand smoke! / tell me how i can tell you i love you without turning into a fucking bore / "the world is all that is the case" / "the world is yours"

Miranda McLeod

TRESPASSER INCIDENT

The conductor tells Cheryl the train has been delayed due to a trespasser incident. He is walking up the aisle, stopping at each occupied seat to lean down and say, quietly, "The train has been delayed due to a trespasser incident." Cheryl's first thought is that she will miss the show. She is meeting her sister in the city and they are seeing a play starring Al Pacino. Tickets were very hard to get.

Cheryl closes her book around her index finger and leans forward. She wants to ask a question. Because her thoughts have shifted now, from the word *delayed* to the word *trespasser*. But already the conductor has moved on. The word sits in the back of her throat like a soft-shelled egg. *Trespasser?* She knows what a trespasser is, of course. She could give an approximate definition. She could pull out her iPhone, which can grab the Internet out of the air wherever she is, and produce Webster's definition. The problem is not definition, then, but context. Here—stalled on the tracks of the New Jersey Transit railway, as out the window a bar of sunlight breaks boldly through the clouds to lay itself on the six bright rails of track, the cushioning gray gravel, the sweet green border of weed that delineates track from the grassy rise that ends in some poor family's noisy yard—*trespasser* is incongruous.

Because, for Cheryl, *trespasser* signals *home*. Home, alone, at night. Awoken. Brought out of the timeless dark of sleep to an immediate dark that remains nameless, formless, as her waking brain casts about, assembling that collection of characteristics that defines her: a woman, in her bedroom, in a house, which she owns, sleeping, alone, because her husband is dead and she is forty pounds overweight.

And there, again: the noise. A noise that woke her but remained elusive, unnamed, as her brain gathered itself into herself. Cheryl. It is only after it sounds a second time that she can identify it for what it is. The creak of a floorboard.

Trespasser. Her mind finds the word and holds it confidently, and she feels immediate relief. As if a vocabulary review is her most urgent task. As if naming something controls it.

Another creak, and a shadow, black on black, sweeping across the floor. Now, understandably, logically, fear crowds her relief. Not completely, though. Vocabulary is that powerful. It is somehow tied up in her brain's ability to register an unheard sound, awake and organize itself into *woman*, in a *house*, which she *owns, sleeping, alone*, because her husband is *dead* and she is *forty pounds overweight*. Vocabulary is important. And context.

But the creak sounds again, the shadow shifts, and just like that the fear presses against her throat. She pushes herself up and back against the headboard and reaches for her nightstand. She's not sure what she's reaching for, but on her nightstand are her glasses, a lamp, and her iPhone. Whichever presents itself first will no doubt save her.

It's the lamp. How she loves that lamp! It is heavy and porcelain, her mother's once, and has two rounded brass cylinders dangling from chains at the neck. She slides her hand up the lamp's breast, finds one of the cylinders, cool and solid, and pulls.

Light floods the room, and with it, sound. Whatever has been creaking her floorboards in the hall starts up a tremendous racket, and as Cheryl fumbles for her glasses and flings back the sheets and rushes toward her door, her first thought is that it must be some sort of animal in her hall, a goat or a small horse, which, frightened by the sudden light, is now bucking and kicking gashes in her wallpaper. But of course not. What sounded to her like hooves is really just the pounding and scuffling of boots, worn by men. Two of them. Startled.

Cheryl meets them in the living room. At the flash of the light they ran, but Cheryl is close behind, her glasses finally on, relief and fear now colored by a strange sort of bravado, which had first allowed her to imagine these men as a furious and troublesome goat, had allowed her to charge after them, but is now fading as she reaches the living room and all three see in the ambient light from the picture window what it is they really are: two men in boots and black clothing and a middle aged lady in bare feet and a nightgown, standing together in a dark living room.

"Suicide!" The word erupts a few feet in front of Cheryl and she is thrust back into herself, her present self, sitting on the stalled train, staring out the window. She blinks. She shifts her eyes to the oily gray fabric of the seat in front of her, and then back out onto the bright rails.

"Suicide!" The word erupts again, and this time, mimicking it, her brain erupts, too, rocketing into her garage. Jim, in the car, motor running. The key to the safety deposit box in his shirt pocket. All those well-ordered papers. Everything taken care of, right down to the funeral arrangements. Nothing for her to do.

"A trespasser *suicide*? What does that even mean?" The voice is coming from the front of the train car. A woman's, aghast. She is an older woman, older than Cheryl, and she is speaking to the conductor, who is leaning over, talking quietly. So this woman, braver, has asked a follow-up question. Cheryl tries to hear the conductor's response, but his voice is too low, almost a whisper. She opens her purse and pulls out her iPhone. She will Google it.

NJ Transit Oct 10 2012. Her hands are shaking and it takes her a long time to type all this in and press *Done*. By the time she's finished, the conductor has moved on and the older lady is conferring with the people near her, splashing her information around. "That's right, *suicide*. That's what he said. Oh, I don't know. I don't know anything about it. Just that he said *incident*, and I said, 'What kind of incident?' and he said *'Suicide*. Trespasser *suicide*.'"

Cheryl's screen flashes. There are results, but nothing helpful, the meaningless Oct and 10 and 2012 of her search scattered across the resulting hits.

10th of March.
Rerouting due to track work for the next 12 days.
Kids dress as transit workers for Halloween.

She adds the word *Trespasser* and puts quotation marks around Oct 10 2012 slowly, laboriously, with the little keypad. Now Google understands.

October 10 2012 – NJ Transit Trespasser Incident Causes Delays
The story is short, just a few lines on a local news station's website.

> A pedestrian was struck and killed by an Amtrak train Saturday afternoon near Edison Station, causing delays to Northeast Corridor service for New Jersey Transit and Amtrak trains.
>
> The 3:49 p.m. fatality, which involved southbound Amtrak Northeast Regional Train 87, was described by NJ Transit as a "trespasser incident."
>
> Vernae Graham, a spokesperson for Amtrak, said the incident happened about a mile and a half east of the Amtrak station in New Brunswick. She said that 215 passengers were on the train at the time, and that none of them were injured, nor were any Amtrak staff injured.

Oh, she thinks. This is what they mean by *trespasser*. The tracks, the whole system of rail lines and stations and trailers and still equipment and signal switches and cushioning gravel and sweet lines of weed—it all belongs to New Jersey Transit. It's all New Jersey Transit's home. It can, in that way, be trespassed.

There is no mention of *suicide* in the article, which is fine by her. She doesn't want to think about *suicide*. The word tugs at something ominous and deep inside her, like a string has been tied around her intestines magically, secretly, so that even she is barely aware that something vital in her is being held hostage. Cheryl closes her eyes and lifts her face, hoping to catch some of the sunlight that is shining onto the tracks, but the angle is wrong. The lids of her eyes remain black. *Trespasser incident.* Nothing about a suicide. She allows *trespasser* to reassert itself. She allows her dark living room to open up again, sees herself gather the remnants of her bravado around her like a robe and stride with what she hopes is a confident, matronly gait to the light switch on the wall.

"Hey!" one of the men says gruffly, stepping forward, but it is too late. She flicks the switch. Again, they shrink from the light. They take a step back, look at each other, and then one of them—the one who spoke—takes two big steps to the picture window and jerks the blinds shut. "That's it. Don't move." He plants himself in front of the window and glares at her, as if she might try to throw herself through the glass. His lips are full and red, like a woman's.

Cheryl is properly, finally, afraid. All bravado, all relief, is gone. She crosses her arms under her breasts, which are loose and hanging. She wishes she did have a robe on, a real one, and a bra. She is aware of her unprotected feet, with their yellowed nails, and her hair, which needs washing and is gathered in a loose, messy braid.

The men, too, seem to feel the shift. One of them—the silent one—strides toward her and a cry fills her throat like a soft-shelled egg. But she stays quiet. Something about the man's face—the firm set of his mouth, the creases that run like scars down his cheeks—tells her that it is best to stay quiet. He grasps her arm above the elbow and spins her around to face the wall. His grip is hard, and she can feel the individual pressure of each of his five fingers. She hears his talkative partner leave the room and go into the kitchen. She hears him jerk open her utensil drawers and slam them shut again. His movements are angry, forceful, and she is reminded of Jim, the way he would slam about when looking for a screwdriver, or getting a glass of water, when he wanted to tell her he was mad about something without actually telling her. Has she made this man, this trespasser, mad? Probably. They'd probably assumed her dark house was empty. They probably did not expect to be chased like goats down the hall.

She hears the man leave the kitchen and walk back toward her. Of course, he is coming to kill her. Of course, he has taken a knife from her kitchen and will now slice her throat. Here, in the corner of her living room. She stares at her wallpaper. It has a pattern of dark green leaves on a cream background. Jim had disliked it, but she'd insisted, seeing in it something stately and faintly British, something her mother would've liked. Once it was up, though, covering the four long walls of the living room and wrapping around into the dining room and the hall, she could see what Jim meant. It was a lot of leaves, spread as they were over such a big space. A lot of dark green for a house with large windows, with blond wooden floors. She had always meant to change it.

Now, with the angry trespasser bearing down on her, she never will. She will die here in the corner of her living room. She is afraid, but fear is not the pressing thing. Fear has been subsumed by a total, encompassing certainty. She will die here in the corner of her living room. And what does fear, or bravado, or vocabulary have to do with that?

She holds one of the dark green leaves tightly in her gaze, narrowing her eyes to cup it. It is heart-shaped, veined, with a tendril curling off into the cream. It is slightly smaller than her palm. It is one leaf out of many leaves. Too many leaves. There is something British about it.

The talkative man steps behind her. She can feel his body close, a few inches away. He raises his arms—of course, the knife. It is now that she will die in the corner of her living room.

But no. He raises his arms and the pressure is not at her throat but at her eyes. It's a dishtowel, being tied roughly around her face. She can tell from the weave, and from the slight moldy, chemical smell, that it is one of her old dishtowels, a stained and torn one she now uses to clean the floorboards and the oven, and sometimes the bathroom. Once it is secure, the silent man jerks her about and pulls her away from the corner, where she did not die.

He leads her to the sofa. She trips on the area rug and, taking offense at her resistance, at her weight dragging against him, he jerks harder. She is thrown onto the sofa. She lays there, unmoving. In her fall, her nightgown has tangled around her waist. She is lying on one hip, facing the back of the sofa. She is aware of her butt, in its wide pink underwear, unveiled, facing the men. The room is silent. Her heart beats quickly, and with each pulse it's as if the egg in her throat pulses too, throbbing in its soft shell. She sees herself as they do: blindfolded, facing the back of the sofa, her nightgown pulled up, her wide, pink butt. Vulnerable. She knows they are all thinking the same thing. Are they the type to rape an old lady? Is she the type of old lady who gets raped?

There is a jolt. A shudder. And the train begins to move. She wonders if that means it's over, if the trespasser has been cleaned up, if the families have been notified. But the train doesn't pick up speed, it inches along, and as the landscape moves slowly past she begins to see evidence of the incident. First, a police car, sitting still, empty, alongside the tracks. Then an unmarked black SUV, a passenger-side door open.

And then the meat, in a flood, a medical examiner's truck, a car stamped CRIME LAB along its door. Two of them, then three, another cop car, but this one with its lights silently, uselessly, flashing. Cops, too, and men dressed not like cops but in official garb, windbreakers and shining shoes, and railway workers in neon vests and hardhats. No paramedics, though. No ambulances. It is all very calm and orderly. Cheryl feels a dull, protective sort of anger at all the order outside her window. There are no tears or rushing about, and there should be. Someone's job at these sorts of crime scenes should be emotional expression. A person should be positioned up the bank, a safe distance away, so that they may scream and rush about without endangering any evidence. This should be an official job, not the task of a grieved wife arriving on the scene, flustering the transit workers, who are not trained to deal with family members, who take her—drag her, really—to a trailer by the side of the tracks and force a cup of tepid water into her hands and ask her, over and over, "How did you get here? Who notified you?" while she clutches the cup of water in one hand and an iPhone in the other with great ropes of snot stretching down her face.

No, an official position, filled by a professional. She has heard that there are places in the Middle East where you can hire mourners for a funeral. Women, professionals, who, for a fee, will do that wonderfully chilling ululation, over and over again, at the top of their lungs. Because even a trespasser deserves some expression of emotion.

It is Cheryl, on the sofa, who breaks the silence. All three of them are still, quiet, waiting in the endless moment when something strikes her: a memory. Of Jim. Jim at a dinner party, at the dining room table, gesticulating with his knife against a backdrop of too-green leaves. *And so I say to him,* he pauses, waits until all eyes are on him, and then stabs the air. *When you come to a fork in the road, take it!* The men around the table guffaw, even though they have no doubt heard Jim quote Yogi Berra before. He's always quoting Yogi Berra. He credits Yogi Berra with much of his success, and Jim is a very successful man. He sells steel, which is less about steel and more about inviting younger salesmen to his home so that he may impress them with his modest house, his modest housewife, and her modest food, all of which make him all the more impressive to his underlings, gurgling on scotch and soda on her couch, laughing too loudly. A rich man who lives cheaply. *Keys to the kingdom,* Jim would say, passing her in the kitchen, swatting her butt with a casual, heavy hand.

Cheryl does not move, only takes a deep breath, forcing it past the throbbing egg, and says into the pillow cushion, "I have some money."

"What?" It's the talkative man.

Cheryl shifts on the couch, turning her head toward the men, rolling so that she is on her back now. "My husband ... there's a safe. With jewelry. And some cash."

She hears the men move, then. They walk to the doorway between the dining room and the living room and speak quietly. She sits up on the couch, pulling her nightgown back down around her thighs.

"The code's simple," she calls out to them. "Yogi Berra's birthday. My husband loved—loves—Yogi Berra."

"Lady," a man says, and it is a new voice, higher. The silent man. "Shut up." But they move, one down the hall to her bedroom, one to the dining room. She hears them rooting around, the clanking of her grandmother's silver as it is dumped out, the opening and closing of closet doors in her bedroom. She sits with her hands in her lap, inhaling the scent of bathroom cleaner, resisting the urge to remove the dishrag. She wonders if she should call out the code, or if they know it already. Maybe one of them is also a Yogi Berra fan.

They don't take long. She hears the front door open, feels the cool air rush into the room and raise the hair along her bare legs. She thinks for a moment that they're gone, that they've left the door open behind them, but then suddenly the air shifts. She stiffens. One of them is standing right in front of her. He bends down, or perhaps crouches, and places both hands on her thighs. She can tell, from the pressure, from the ten thick fingers, that it is the silent man touching her. Squeezing her.

"We have your license and your keys. Do not call the police." His hands are hot and hard on her thighs. His breath smells like spearmint. "It's been a lucky night. Don't fuck it up."

When she speaks, her voice is very small, coming from somewhere deep down in her stomach. "My husband will be home soon."

He lifts his hands. "Your husband's dead. Google it."

She sits on her couch with the dishtowel around her eyes for three more minutes. Even though they didn't tell her to do this, she counts out all one hundred and eighty seconds. With each number there is a pull, sharp and insistent, deep inside her. A tugging in her stomach that throbs with the beat of her counting. *Sixty-three*. Tug. *Sixty-four.* Tug. "Your husband's dead," the silent man had said. But he hadn't said, "killed himself." He hadn't said, "suicide." That's something, because for months, ever since Jim's death, she's been doing her best to get a handle on that word. She's doing her best to shake out Jim's death, air it out, bleach it in the sun so that *suicide* fades and fades. It will just take some time, and a careful choice of words.

Cheryl unties the towel and stands up. She closes and locks the front door and walks slowly around her house, assessing the damage. She will make a list of things in need of repair or replacement. She will program the safe with a new combination. Already the pain in her stomach is fading.

"I just don't know how you could do it, commit suicide like that, with a train." The woman at the front of the car is talking loudly again, or maybe she never stopped. "A bit selfish really. All those people inconvenienced. And think of the conductor. Think of how it is on *him*."

Cheryl checks her phone. They were delayed eighteen minutes. She will make the play. But the woman is right, of course. Think of the conductor. Think of the wife, who may have only a few minutes left in her familiar, quiet life. Selfish is the only word for it, and yet, somehow, it doesn't quite fit. The definition is wrong. Or maybe the context.

The train picks up speed. The rails glint now, running like narrow channels of water alongside Cheryl's window, and the green of the grass and trees bordering the tracks begins to soften into something like fabric. Contented, the woman in the front of the car quiets, satisfied, no doubt, in the small part she was able to play in getting them all going. They are past the investigation now, past the site of the incident, and they can move quickly again through the landscape.

Jess Dutschmann

HERE IS YOUR POEM ABOUT MY INSIDES

Over the
summer I
was also
sick. I get guilty, then I get angry, then I get angry for being guilty,
squashed visibly
then I remember again.

HOC ACCIDENS

You didn't listen and summoned
him anyway and now look at
this mess you have made

all the little girls screaming
all the little boys dancing
they should not be dancing

a ruby hawk's going to
catch you by the throat
and feed you to her babies

the hawk is named for
dark tongues and silent poetry
and I will not warn you when it comes.

SAMUEL TOLZMANN GRACE

Elena Ferrante

FROM THE STORY OF A NEW NAME

Translated by Ann Goldstein

We disembarked on the island the second Sunday in July, Stefano and Lila, Rino and Pinuccia, Nunzia and I. The two men, loaded down with bags, were apprehensive, like ancient heroes in an unknown land, uneasy without the armor of their cars, unhappy that they had had to rise early and forgo the neighborhood leisureliness of their day off. The wives, dressed in their Sunday best, were annoyed with them but in different ways: Pinuccia because Rino was too encumbered to pay attention to her, Lila because Stefano pretended to know what he was doing and where he was going, when it was clear that he didn't. As for Nunzia, she had the appearance of someone who feels that she is barely tolerated, and she was careful not to say anything inappropriate that might annoy the young people. The only one who was truly content was me, with a bag over my shoulder that held my few things, excited by the smells of Ischia, the sounds, the colors that, as soon as I got off the boat, corresponded precisely to the memories of that earlier vacation.

We arranged ourselves in two mini cabs, jammed-in bodies, sweat, luggage. The house, rented in a hurry with the help of a *salumi* supplier of Ischian origin, was on the road that led to a place called Cuotto. It was a simple structure and belonged to a cousin of the supplier, a thin woman, over sixty, unmarried, who greeted us with brusque efficiency. Stefano and Rino dragged the suitcases up a narrow staircase, joking but also cursing because of the effort. The owner led us into shadowy rooms stuffed with sacred images and small, glowing lamps. But when we opened the windows we saw, beyond the road, beyond the vineyards, beyond the palms and pine trees, a long strip of the sea. Or rather: the bedrooms that Pinuccia and Lila took—after some friction of the *yours is bigger; no, yours is bigger* type—faced the sea, while the room that fell to Nunzia had a sort of porthole, high up, so that we never discovered what was outside it, and mine, which was very small, and barely had space for the bed, looked out on a chicken coop sheltered by a forest of reeds.

There was nothing to eat in the house. On the advice of the owner we went to a trattoria, which was dark and had no other customers. We sat down dubiously, just to get fed, but in the end even Nunzia, who was distrustful of all cooking that was not her own, found that it was good and wanted to take something home so that she could prepare dinner that evening. Stefano didn't make the slightest move to ask for the check, and, after a mute hesitation, Rino resigned himself to paying for everyone. At that point we girls proposed going to see the beach, but the two men resisted, yawned, said they were tired. We insisted, especially Lila. "We ate too much," she said, "it'll do us good to walk, the beach is right here, do you feel like it, Mamma?"

After a bored stroll through the rooms, both Stefano and Rino, almost in unison, said they wanted to have a little nap. They laughed, whispered to each other, laughed again, and then nodded at their wives, who followed them unwillingly into the bedrooms. Nunzia and I remained alone for a couple of hours. We inspected the state of the kitchen and found it dirty, which led Nunzia to start washing everything carefully: plates, glasses, silverware, pots. It was a struggle to get her to let me help. She asked me to keep track of a number of urgent requests for the owner, and when she herself lost count of the things that were needed, she marveled that I was able to remember everything, saying, "That's why you're so clever at school."

Finally the two couples reappeared, first Stefano and Lila, then Rino and Pinuccia. I again proposed going to see the beach, but there was coffee, joking, chatting, and Nunzia, who began to cook, and Pinuccia, who was clinging to Rino, making him feel her stomach, murmuring, stay, leave tomorrow morning, and so the time flew and yet again we did nothing. In the end the men had to rush, afraid of missing the ferry and, cursing because they hadn't brought their cars, had to find someone to take them to the Port. They disappeared almost without saying goodbye. Pinuccia burst into tears.

In silence we girls began to unpack the bags, to arrange our things, while Nunzia insisted on making the bathroom shine. Only when we were sure that the men had not missed the ferry and would not return did we relax, begin to joke. We had ahead of us a long week and only ourselves to worry about. Pinuccia said she was afraid of being alone in her room—there was an image of a grieving Madonna with knives in her heart that sparkled in the lamplight—and went to sleep with Lila. I shut myself in my little room to enjoy my secret: *Nino was in Forio, not far away*, and maybe even the next day I would meet him on the beach. I felt wild, reckless, but I was glad about it. There was a part of me that was sick of being a sensible person.

It was hot; I opened the window. I listened to the chickens pecking, the rustle of the reeds; then I became aware of the mosquitoes. I closed the window quickly and spent at least an hour going after them and crushing them with one of the books that Professor Galiani had lent me, *Complete Plays*, by a writer named Samuel Beckett. I didn't want Nino to see me on the beach with red spots on my face and body; I didn't want him to catch me with a book of plays—for one thing, I had never set foot in a theater. I put aside Beckett, stained by the black or bloody silhouettes of the mosquitoes, and began to read a very complicated text on the idea of nationhood. I fell asleep reading.

In the morning Nunzia, who felt committed to looking after us, went in search of a place to do the shopping, and we headed to the beach, the beach of Citara, which for that entire long vacation we thought was called Cetara.

What pretty bathing suits Lila and Pinuccia displayed when they took off their sundresses: one-piece, of course. The husbands, who as fiancés had been indulgent, especially Stefano, now were against the two-piece; but the colors of the new fabrics were shiny, and the shape of the neckline, front and back, ran elegantly over their skin. I, under an old long-sleeved blue dress, wore the same faded bathing suit, now shapeless, that Nella Incardo had made for me years earlier, at Barano. I undressed reluctantly.

We walked a long way in the sun, until we saw steam rising from some thermal baths, then turned back. Pinuccia and I stopped often to swim; Lila didn't, although she was there for that purpose. Of course, there was no Nino, and I was disappointed; I had been convinced that he would show up, as if by a miracle. When the other two wanted to go back to the house, I stayed on the beach, and walked along the shore toward Forio. That night I was so sunburned that I felt I had a high fever; the skin on my shoulders blistered and for the next few days I had to stay in the house. I cleaned, cooked, and read, and my energy pleased Nunzia, who couldn't stop praising me. Every night, with the excuse that I had been in the house all day to stay out of the sun, I made Lila and Pina walk to Forio, which was some distance away. We wandered through the town, had some ice cream. It's pretty here, Pinuccia complained, and it's a morgue where we are. But for me Forio was also a morgue: Nino had not appeared.

Toward the end of the week I proposed to Lila that we should visit

Barano and the Maronti. Lila agreed enthusiastically, and Pinuccia didn't want to stay and be bored with Nunzia. We left early. Under our dresses we wore our bathing suits, and in a bag I carried our towels, sandwiches, a bottle of water. My stated purpose was to take advantage of that trip to say hello to Nella, Maestra Oliviero's cousin, whom I had stayed with during my summer on Ischia. The secret plan, instead, was to see the Sarratore family and get from Marisa the address of the friend with whom Nino was staying in Forio. I was naturally afraid of running into the father, Donato, but I hoped that he was at work; and, in order to see the son, I was ready to run the risk of having to endure some obscene remark from him.

When Nella opened the door and I stood before her, like a ghost, she was stunned, tears came to her eyes. "It's happiness," she said, apologizing.

But it wasn't only that. I had reminded her of her cousin, who, she told me, wasn't comfortable in Potenza, was ill and wasn't getting better. She led us out to the terrace, offered us whatever we wanted, was very concerned with Pinuccia and her pregnancy. She made her sit down, wanted to touch her stomach, which protruded a little. Meanwhile I made Lila go on a sort of pilgrimage: I showed her the corner of the terrace where I had spent so much time in the sun, the place where I sat at the table, the corner where I made my bed at night. For a fraction of a second I saw Donato leaning over me as he slid his hand under the sheets, touched me. I felt revulsion but this didn't keep me from asking Nella casually, "And the Sarratores?"

"They're at the beach."

"How's it going this year?"

"Ah, well . . . "

"They're too demanding?"

"Ever since he became more the journalist than the railroad worker, yes."

"Is he here?"

"He's on sick leave."

"And is Marisa here?"

"No, not Marisa, but except for her they're all here."

"All?"

"You understand."

"No, I swear, I don't understand anything."

She laughed heartily.

"Nino's here today, too, Lenù. When he needs money he shows up for half a day, then he goes back to stay with a friend who has a house in Forio."

We left Nella, and went down to the beach with our things. Lila teased me mildly the whole way. "You're sneaky," she said, "you made me come to Ischia just because Nino's here, admit it." I wouldn't admit it, I defended myself. Then Pinuccia joined her sister-in-law, in a coarser tone, and accused me of having compelled her to make a long and tiring journey to Barano for my own purposes, without taking her pregnancy into account. From then on I denied it even more firmly, and in fact I threatened them both. I promised that if they said anything improper in the presence of the Sarratores I would take the boat and return to Naples that night.

I immediately picked out the family. They were in exactly the same place where they used to settle years before, and had the same umbrella, the same bathing suits, the same bags, the same way of basking in the sun: Donato belly up in the black sand, leaning on his elbows; his wife, Lidia, sitting on a towel and leafing through a magazine. To my great disappointment Nino wasn't under the umbrella. I scanned the water and glimpsed a dark dot that appeared and disappeared on the rocking surface of the sea: I hoped it was him. Then I announced myself, calling aloud to Pino, Clelia, and Ciro, who were playing on the shore.

Ciro had grown; he didn't recognize me, and smiled uncertainly. Pino and Clelia ran toward me excitedly, and the parents turned to look, out of curiosity. Lidia jumped up, shouting my name and waving; Sarratore hurried toward me with a big welcoming smile and open arms. I avoided his embrace, saying only Hello, how are you. They were very friendly; I introduced Lila and Pinuccia, mentioned their parents, said whom they had married. Donato immediately focused on the two girls. He began addressing them respectfully as Signora Carracci and Signora Cerullo; he remembered them as children. He began, with fatuous elaboration, to speak of time's flight. I talked to Lidia, asked politely about the children and especially Marisa. Pino, Clelia, and Ciro were doing well and it was obvious; they immediately gathered around me, waiting for the right moment to draw me into their games. As for Marisa, her mother said that she had stayed in Naples with her aunt and uncle; she had to retake exams in four subjects in September and had to go to private lessons. "Serves her right," she said darkly. "She didn't work all year, now she deserves to suffer."

I said nothing, but I doubted that Marisa was suffering: she would spend the whole summer with Alfonso in the store in Piazza dei Martiri, and I was happy for her. I noticed instead that Lidia bore deep traces of grief: in her face, which was losing its contours, in her eyes, in her shrunken breast, in her heavy stomach. All the time we talked she was glancing fearfully at her husband, who, playing the role of the kindly man, was devoting himself to Lila and Pinuccia. She stopped paying attention to me and kept her eyes glued to him when he offered to take them swimming, promising Lila that he would teach her to swim. "I taught all my children," we heard him say, "I'll teach you, too."

I never asked about Nino, nor did Lidia ever mention him. But now the black dot in the sparkling blue of the sea stopped moving out. It reversed direction, grew larger, I began to distinguish the white of the foam exploding beside it.

Yes, it's him, I thought anxiously.

Nino emerged from the water looking with curiosity at his father, who was holding Lila afloat with one arm and with the other was showing her what to do. Even when he saw me and recognized me, he continued to frown.

"What are you doing here?" he asked.

"I'm on vacation," I answered, "and I came by to see Signora Nella."

He looked again with annoyance in the direction of his father and the two girls.

"Isn't that Lina?"

"Yes, and that's her sister-in-law Pinuccia. I don't know if you remember her."

He rubbed his hair with the towel, continuing to stare at the three in the water. I told him almost breathlessly that we would be staying on Ischia until September, that we had a house not far from Forio, that Lila's mother was there, too, that on Sunday the husbands of Lila and Pinuccia would come. As I spoke it seemed to me that he wasn't even listening, but still I said, and in spite of Lidia's presence, that on the weekend I had nothing to do.

"Come see us," he said, and then he spoke to his mother: "I have to go."

"Already?"

"I have things to do."

"Elena's here."

Nino looked at me as if he had become aware of my presence only then. He rummaged in his shirt, which was hanging on the umbrella, took out a pencil and a notebook, wrote something, tore out the page, and handed it to me.

"I'm at this address," he said.

Clear, decisive as a movie actor. I took the page as if it were a holy relic.

"Eat something first," his mother begged him. He didn't answer.

"And at least wave goodbye to Papa."

He changed out of his bathing suit, wrapping a towel around his waist, and went off along the shore without saying goodbye to anyone.

We spent the entire day at the Maronti, I playing and swimming with the children, Pinuccia and Lila completely occupied by Donato, who took them for a walk all the way to the thermal baths. At the end Pinuccia was exhausted, and Sarratore showed us a convenient and pleasant way of going home. We went to a hotel that was built practically over the water, as if on stilts, and there, for a few lire, we got a boat, entrusting ourselves to an old sailor.

As soon as we set out, Lila said sarcastically, "Nino didn't give you much encouragement."

"He had to study."

"And he couldn't even say hello?"

"That's how he is."

"How he is is rude," Pinuccia interjected. "He's as rude as the father is nice."

They were both convinced that Nino hadn't been polite or pleasant, and I let them think it; I preferred prudently to keep my secrets. And it seemed to me that if they thought he was disdainful of even a really good student like me, they would more easily put up with the fact that he had ignored them and maybe they would even forgive him. I wanted to protect him from their rancor, and I succeeded: they seemed to forget about him right away, Pinuccia was enthusiastic about Sarratore's graciousness, and Lila said with satisfaction, "He taught me to float, and even how to swim. He's great."

The sun was setting. I thought of Donato's molestations, and shuddered. From the violet sky came a chilly dampness. I said to Lila, "He's the one who wrote that the panel in the Piazza dei Martiri shop was ugly."

Pinuccia had a smug expression of agreement.

Lila said, "He was right."

I became upset. "And he's the one who ruined Melina."

Lila answered, with a laugh, "Or maybe he made her feel good for once."

That remark wounded me. I knew what Melina had endured, what her children endured. I also knew Lidia's sufferings, and how Sarratore, behind his fine manners, hid a desire that respected nothing and no one. Nor had I forgotten that Lila, since she was a child, had witnessed the torments of the widow Cappuccio and how painful it had been for her. So what was this tone, what were those words—a signal to me? Did she want to say to me: you're a girl, you don't know anything about a woman's needs? I abruptly changed my mind about the secrecy of my secrets. I wanted immediately to show that I was a woman like them and knew.

176

"Nino gave me his address," I said to Lila. "If you don't mind, when Stefano and Rino come I'm going to see him."

Address. Go see him. Bold formulations. Lila narrowed her eyes; a sharp line crossed her forehead. Pinuccia had a malicious look, she touched Lila's knee. She laughed: "You hear? Lenuccia has a date tomorrow. And she has the address."

I flushed.

"Well, if you're with your husbands, what am I supposed to do?"

For a long moment there was only the noise of the engine and the mute presence of the sailor at the helm.

Lila said coldly, "Keep Mamma company. I didn't bring you here to have fun."

I restrained myself. We had had a week of freedom. That day, besides, both she and Pinuccia, on the beach, in the sun, during long swims, and thanks to the words that Sarratore knew how to use to inspire laughter and to charm, had forgotten themselves. Donato had made them feel like girl-women in the care of an unusual father, the rare father who doesn't punish you but encourages you to express your desires without guilt. And now that the day was over I, in declaring that I would have a Sunday to myself with a university student—what was I doing, was I reminding them both that their week of not being wives was over and that their husbands were about to reappear? Yes, I had overdone it. Cut out your tongue, I thought.

The husbands, in fact, arrived early. They were expected Sunday morning, but they appeared Saturday evening, very excited, with Lambrettas that they had, I think, rented at the Ischia Port. Nunzia prepared a lavish dinner. There was talk of the neighborhood, of the stores, of how the new shoes were coming along. Rino was full of self-praise for the models he was perfecting with his father, but at an opportune moment he thrust some sketches under Lila's nose, and she examined them reluctantly, suggesting some modifications. Then we sat down at the table, and the two young men gorged themselves, competing to see who could eat more. It wasn't even ten when they dragged their wives to the bedrooms.

I helped Nunzia clear and wash the dishes. Then I shut myself in my room. I read a little. The heat in the closed room was suffocating, but I was afraid of the blotches I'd get from the mosquito bites, and I didn't open the window. I tossed and turned in the bed, soaked with sweat: I thought of Lila, of how, slowly, she had yielded. Certainly, she didn't show any particular affection for her husband; and the tenderness that I had sometimes seen in her gestures when they were engaged had disappeared. During dinner she had frequently commented with disgust at the way Stefano gobbled his food, the way he drank; but it was evident that some equilibrium, who knows how precarious, had been reached. When he, after some allusive remarks, headed toward the bedroom, Lila followed without delay, without saying go on, I'll join you later; she was resigned to an inevitable routine. Between her and her husband there was not the carnival spirit displayed by Rino and Pinuccia, but there was no resistance, either. Deep into the night I heard the noise of the two couples, the laughter and the sighs, the doors opening, the water coming out of the tap, the whirlpool of the flush, the doors closing. Finally I fell asleep.

On Sunday I had breakfast with Nunzia. I waited until ten for any of them to emerge; they didn't; I went to the beach. I stayed until noon and no one came. I went back to the house, Nunzia told me that the two couples had gone for a tour of the island on the Lambrettas, advising us not to wait for them for lunch. In fact they returned around three, slightly drunk, sunburned, all four full of enthusiasm for Casamicciola, Lacco Ameno, Forio. The two girls had shining eyes and immediately glanced at me slyly.

"Lenù," Pinuccia almost shouted, "guess what happened."

"What."

"We met Nino on the beach," Lila said. My heart stopped.

"Oh."

"My goodness, he is really a good swimmer," Pinuccia said excitedly, cutting the air with exaggerated arm strokes.

And Rino: "He's not unlikable: he was interested in how shoes are made."

And Stefano: "He has a friend named Soccavo, and he's the mortadella Soccavo: his father owns a sausage factory in San Giovanni a Teduccio."

And Rino again: "That guy's got money."

And again Stefano: "Forget the student, Lenù, he doesn't have a lira: aim for Soccavo, you'd be better off."

After a little more joking (*Would you look at that, Lenuccia is about to be the richest of all, She seems like a good girl and yet*), they withdrew again into the bedrooms.

I was incredibly disappointed. They had met Nino, gone swimming with him, talked to him, and without me. I put on my best dress—the same one, the one I'd worn to the wedding, even though it was hot—I carefully combed my hair, which had become very blond in the sun, and told Nunzia I was going for a walk.

I walked to Forio, uneasy because of the long, solitary distance, because of the heat, because of the uncertain result of my undertaking.

I tracked down the address of Nino's friend, I called several times from the street, fearful that he wouldn't answer.

"Nino, Nino."

He looked out.

"Come up."

"I'll wait here."

I waited, I was afraid that he would treat me rudely. Instead he came out of the doorway with an unusually friendly expression. How disturbing his angular face was. And how pleasantly crushed I felt confronted by his long profile, his broad shoulders and narrow chest, that taut skin, the sole, dark covering of his thinness, merely bones, muscles, tendons. He said his friend would join us later; we walked through the center of Forio, amid the Sunday market stalls. He asked me about the bookstore on Mezzocannone. I told him that Lila had asked me to go with her on vacation and so I had quit. I didn't mention the fact that she was giving me money, as if going with her were a job, as if I were her employee. I asked him about Nadia, he said only: "Everything's fine." "Do you write to each other?" "Yes." "Every day?" "Every week." That was our conversation, already we had nothing more of ourselves to share. We don't know anything about each other, I thought. Maybe I could ask how relations are with his father, but in what tone? And, besides, didn't I see with my own eyes that they were bad? Silence: I felt awkward.

But he promptly shifted onto the only terrain that seemed to justify our meeting. He said he was glad to see me, all he could talk about with his friend was soccer and exam subjects. He praised me. Professor Galiani perceived it, he said, you're the only girl in the school who has any curiosity about things that aren't useful for exams and grades. He started to speak about serious subjects, we resorted immediately to a fine, impassioned Italian at which we knew we excelled. He started off with the problem of violence. He mentioned a peace demonstration in Cortona and related it skillfully to the beatings that had taken place in a piazza in Turin. He said he wanted to understand more about the link between immigration and industry. I agreed, but what did I know about those things? Nothing. Nino realized it, and he told me in great detail about an uprising of young southerners and the harshness with which the police had repressed them. "They call them *napoli*, they call them Moroccans, they call them Fascists, provocateurs, anarcho-syndicalists. But really they are boys about whom no institution cares, so neglected that when they get angry they destroy everything." Searching for something to say that would please him, I ventured, "If you don't have a solid knowledge of the problems and if you don't find lasting solutions, then naturally violence breaks out. But the people who rebel aren't to blame, it's the ones who don't know how to govern." He gave me an admiring look, and said, "That's exactly what I think."

I was really pleased. I felt encouraged and cautiously went on to some reflections on how to reconcile individuality and universality, drawing on Rousseau and other memories of the readings imposed by Professor Galiani. Then I asked, "Have you read Federico Chabod?"

I mentioned that name because he was the author of the book on the idea of nationhood that I had read a few pages of. I didn't know anything else, but at school I had learned to give the impression that I knew a lot. *Have you read Federico Chabod?* It was the only moment when Nino seemed to be annoyed. I realized that he didn't know who Chabod was and from that I got an electrifying sensation of fullness. I began to summarize the little I had learned, but I quickly realized that to know, to compulsively display what he knew, was his point of strength and at the same time his weakness. He felt strong if he took the lead and weak if he lacked words. He darkened, in fact he stopped me almost immediately. He sidetracked the conversation; he started talking about the Regions, about how urgent it was to get them approved, about autonomy and decentralization, about economic planning on a regional basis, all things I had never heard a word about. No Chabod, then: I left him the field. And I liked to hear him talk, read the passion in his face. His eyes brightened when he was excited.

We went on like that for at least an hour. Isolated from the shouting around us, its coarse dialect, we felt exclusive, he and I alone, with our vigilant Italian, with those conversations that mattered to us and no one else. What were we doing? A discussion? Practicing for future confrontations with people who had learned to use words as we had? An exchange of signals to prove to ourselves that such words were the basis of a long and fruitful friendship? A cultivated screen for sexual desire? I don't know. I certainly had no particular passion for those subjects, for the real things and people they referred to. I had no training, no habit, only the usual desire not to make a bad showing. It was wonderful, though—that is certain. I felt the way I did at the end of the year when I saw the list of my grades and read: passed. But I also understood that there was no comparison with the exchanges I had had with Lila years earlier, which ignited my brain, and in the course of which we tore the words from each other's mouth, creating an excitement that seemed like a storm of electrical charges. With Nino it was different. I felt that I had to pay attention to say what he wanted me to say, hiding from him both my ignorance and the few things that I knew and he didn't. I did this, and felt proud that he was trusting me with his convictions. But now something else happened. Suddenly he said, That's enough, grabbed my hand, exclaimed, like a fluorescent caption, *Now I'll take you to see a landscape that you'll never forget*, and dragged me to Piazza del Soccorso without letting go, rather, he entwined his fingers in mine, so that, overwhelmed as I was by his clasp, I preserve no memory of the arc of the deep blue sea.

It truly overwhelmed me. Once or twice he disentangled his fingers to smooth his hair, but he immediately took my hand again. I wondered for a moment how he reconciled that intimate gesture with his bond with Professor Galiani's daughter. Maybe for him, I answered, it's merely how he thinks of the friendship between male and female. But the kiss on Via Mezzocannone? That, too, was nothing, new customs, new habits of youth; and anyway so slight, just the briefest contact. I should be satisfied with the happiness of right now, the chance of this vacation that I wanted: later I'll lose him, he'll leave, he has a destiny that can in no way be mine, too.

I was absorbed by these throbbing thoughts when I heard a roar behind me and noisy cries of my name. Rino and Stefano passed us at full speed on their Lambrettas, with their wives behind. They slowed down, turned back with a skillful maneuver. I let go of Nino's hand.

"And your friend?" Stefano asked, revving his engine.

"He'll be here soon."

"Say hello from me."

"Yes."

Rino asked, "Do you want to take Lenuccia for a spin?"

"No, thanks."

"Come on, you see she'd like to."

Nino flushed, he said, "I don't know how to ride a Lambretta."

"It's easy, like a bicycle."

"I know, but it's not for me."

Stefano laughed: "Rinù, he's a guy who studies, forget it."

I had never seen him so lighthearted. Lila sat close against him, with both arms around his waist. She urged him, "Let's go, if you don't hurry you'll miss the boat."

"Yes, let's go," cried Stefano, "tomorrow we have to work: not like you people who sit in the sun and go swimming. Bye, Lenù, bye, Nino. Be good boys and girls."

"Nice to meet you," Rino said cordially.

They went off; Lila waved goodbye to Nino, shouting, "Please, take her home."

She's acting like my mother, I thought with a little annoyance, she's playing grownup.

Nino took me by the hand again and said, "Rino is nice, but why did Lina marry that moron?"

A little later I also met his friend, Bruno Soccavo, who was around twenty, and very short, with a low forehead, black curly hair, a pleasant face but scarred by what must have been severe acne.

They walked me home, beside the wine-colored sea of twilight. Nino didn't take my hand again, even though Bruno left us practically alone: he went in front or lingered behind, as if he didn't want to disturb us. Since Soccavo never said a word to me, I didn't speak to him, either, his shyness made me shy. But when we parted, at the house, it was he who asked suddenly, "Will we meet tomorrow?" And Nino found out where we were going to the beach, he insisted on precise directions. I gave them.

"Are you going in the morning or the afternoon?"

"Morning and afternoon. Lina is supposed to swim a lot."

He promised they would come and see us.

I ran happily up the stairs of the house, but as soon as I came in Pinuccia began to tease me.

"Mamma," she said to Nunzia during dinner, "Lenuccia's going out with the poet's son, a skinny fellow with long hair, who thinks he's better than everybody."

"It's not true."

"It's very true, we saw you holding hands."

Nunzia didn't understand the teasing and took the thing with the earnest gravity that characterized her.

"What does Sarratore's son do?"

"University student."

"Then if you love each other you'll have to wait."

"There's nothing to wait for, Signora Nunzia, we're only friends."

"But if, let's say, you should happen to become engaged, he'll have to finish his studies first, then he'll have to find a job that's worthy of him, and only when he's found something will you be able to get married."

Here Lila interrupted, amused: "She's telling you you'll get moldy."

But Nunzia reproached her: "You mustn't speak like that to Lenuccia." And to console me she said that she had married Fernando at twenty-one, that she had had Rino at twenty-three. Then she turned to her daughter, and said, without malice, only to point out how things stood, "You, on the other hand, were married too young." That comment infuriated Lila and she went to her room. When Pinuccia knocked on the door, to go in to sleep, she yelled not to bother her, "you have your room." How in that atmosphere could I say: Nino and Bruno promised they'd come and see me on the beach? I gave it up. If it happens, I thought, fine, and if it doesn't why tell them. Nunzia, meanwhile, patiently invited her daughter-in-law into her bed, telling her not to be upset by her daughter's nerves.

The night wasn't enough to soothe Lila. On Monday she got up in a worse mood than when she had gone to bed. It's the absence of her husband, Nunzia said apologetically, but neither Pinuccia nor I believed it. I soon discovered that she was angry mainly at me. On the road to the beach she made me carry her bag, and once we were at the beach she sent me back twice, first to get her a scarf, then because she needed some nail scissors. When I gave signs of protest she nearly reminded me of the money she was giving me. She stopped in time, but not so that I didn't understand: it was like when someone is about to hit you and then doesn't.

It was a very hot day; we stayed in the water. Lila practiced hard to keep afloat and made me stand next to her so that I could hold her up if necessary. Yet her spitefulness continued. She kept reproaching me, she said that it was stupid to trust me: I didn't even know how to swim, how could I teach her. She missed Sarratore's talents as an instructor, she made me swear that the next day we would go back to the Maronti. Still, by trial and error, she made a lot of progress. She learned every movement instantly. Thanks to that ability she had learned to make shoes, to dexterously slice salami and provolone, to cheat on the weight. She was born like that; she could have learned the art of engraving merely by studying the gestures of a goldsmith and then been able to work the gold better than he. Already she had stopped gasping for breath, and was forcing composure on every motion: it was as if she were drawing her body on the transparent surface of the sea. Long, slender arms and legs hit the water in a tranquil rhythm, without raising foam like Nino, without the ostentatious tension of Sarratore the father.

"Is this right?"

"Yes."

It was true. In a few hours she could swim better than I could, not to mention Pinuccia, and already she was making fun of our clumsiness.

That bullying air dissipated abruptly when, around four in the afternoon, Nino, who was very tall, and Bruno, who came up to his shoulders, appeared on the beach, just as a cool wind rose, taking away the desire to swim.

Pinuccia was the first to make them out as they advanced along the shore, among the children playing with shovels and pails. She burst out laughing in surprise and said: Look who's coming, the long and the short of it. Nino and his friend, towels over their shoulder, cigarettes and lighters, advanced deliberately, looking for us among the bathers.

I had a sudden sense of power. I shouted, I waved to signal our presence. So Nino had kept his promise. So he had felt, already, the next day, the need to see me again. So he had come purposely from Forio, dragging along his mute companion, and since he had nothing in common with Lila and Pinuccia, it was obvious that he had taken that walk just for me, who alone was not married, or even engaged. I felt happy, and the more my happiness seemed justified—Nino spread his towel next to me, he sat down, he pointed to an edge of the blue fabric, and I, who was the only one sitting on the sand, quickly moved over—the more cordial and talkative I became.

Lila and Pinuccia instead were silent. They stopped teasing me; they stopped squabbling with each other; they listened to Nino as he told funny stories about how he and his friend had organized their life of study.

It was a while before Pinuccia ventured a few words, in a mixture of dialect and Italian. She said the water was nice and warm, that the man who sold fresh coconut hadn't come by yet, that she had a great desire for some. But Nino paid little attention, absorbed in his witty stories, and it was Bruno, more attentive, who felt it his duty not to ignore what a pregnant woman was saying: worried that the child might be born with a craving for coconut, he offered to go in search of some. Pinuccia liked his voice, choked by shyness but kind, the voice of a person who doesn't want to hurt anyone, and she eagerly began chatting with him, in a low voice, as if not to disturb.

Lila, however, remained silent. She took little interest in the platitudes that Pinuccia and Bruno were exchanging, but she didn't miss a word of what Nino and I were saying. That attention made me uneasy, and a few times I said I would be glad to take a walk to the fumaroles, hoping that Nino would say: let's go. But he had just begun to talk about the construction chaos on Ischia, so he agreed mechanically, then continued talking anyway. He dragged Bruno into it, maybe upset by the fact that he was talking to Pinuccia, and called on him as a witness to certain eyesores right next to his parents' house. Nino had a great need to express himself, to summarize his reading, to give shape to what he had himself observed. It was his way of putting his thoughts in order—talk, talk, talk—but certainly, I thought, also a sign of solitude. I proudly felt that I was like him, with the same desire to give myself an educated identity, to impose it, to say: Here's what I know, here's what I'm going to be. But Nino didn't leave me space to do it, even if occasionally, I have to say, I tried. I sat and listened to him, like the others, and when Pinuccia and Bruno exclaimed, "All right, we're going for a walk now, we're going to look for coconut," I gazed insistently at Lila, hoping that she would go with her sister-in-law, leaving me and Nino finally alone to face each other, side by side, on the same towel. But she didn't breathe, and when Pina realized that she was compelled to go for a walk by herself with a young man who was polite but nevertheless unknown, she asked me, in annoyance, "Lenù, come on, don't you want to walk?" I answered, "Yes, but let us finish our conversation, then maybe we'll join you." And she, displeased, went with Bruno toward the fumaroles: they were exactly the same height.

We continued to talk about how Naples and Ischia and all Campania had ended up in the hands of the worst people, who acted like the best people. "Marauders," Nino called them, his voice rising, "destroyers, bloodsuckers, people who steal suitcases of money and don't pay taxes: builders, lawyers for builders, Camorrists, monarcho-fascists, and Christian Democrats who behave as if cement were mixed in Heaven, and God himself, with an enormous trowel, were throwing blocks of it on the hills, on the coasts." But that the three of us were talking is an exaggeration. It was mainly he who talked, every so often I threw in some fact I had read in *Cronache Meridionali*. As for Lila, she spoke only once, and cautiously, when in the list of villains he included shopkeepers.

She asked, "Who are shopkeepers?"

Nino stopped in the middle of a sentence, looked at her in astonishment.

"Tradesmen."

"And why do you call them shopkeepers?"

"That's what they're called."

"My husband is a shopkeeper."

"I didn't mean to offend you."

"I'm not offended."

"Do you pay taxes?"

"I've never heard of them till now."

"Really?"

"Yes."

"Taxes are important for planning the economic life of a community."

"If you say so. You remember Pasquale Peluso?"

"No."

"He's a construction worker. Without all that cement he would lose his job."

"Ah."

"But he's a Communist. His father, also a Communist, in the court's opinion murdered my father-in-law, who had made money on the black market and as a loan shark. And Pasquale is like his father, he has never agreed on the question of peace, not even with the Communists, his comrades. But, even though my husband's money comes directly from my father-in-law's money, Pasquale and I are close friends."

"I don't understand what you're getting at."

Lila made a self-mocking face.

"I don't, either. I was hoping to understand by listening to the two of you."

That was it; she said nothing else. But in speaking she hadn't used her normal aggressive tone of voice, she seriously seemed to want us to help her understand, since the life of the neighborhood was a tangled skein. She had spoken in dialect most of the time, as if to indicate, modestly: I don't use tricks, I speak as I am. And she had summarized disparate things frankly, without seeking, as she usually did, a thread that would hold them together. And in fact neither she nor I had ever heard that word-formula loaded with cultural and political contempt: shopkeepers. And in fact neither she nor I knew anything about taxes: our parents, friends, boyfriends, husbands, relatives acted as if they didn't exist, and school taught nothing that had to do even vaguely with politics. Yet Lila still managed to disrupt what had until that moment been a new and thrilling afternoon. Right after that exchange, Nino tried to return to his subject but he faltered, he went back to telling funny anecdotes about life with Bruno. He said they ate only fried eggs and salami; he said that they drank a lot of wine. Then he seemed embarrassed by his own stories and appeared relieved when Pinuccia and Bruno, their hair wet, came back, eating coconut.

"That was really fun," Pina exclaimed, but with the air of one who wants to say: You two bitches, you sent me off by myself with someone I don't even know.

When the two boys left I walked with them a little way, just to make it clear that they were my friends and had come because of me.

Nino said moodily, "Lina really got lost, what a shame."

I nodded yes, said goodbye, stood for a while with my feet in the water to calm myself.

When we got home, Pinuccia and I were lively, Lila thoughtful. Pinuccia told Nunzia about the visit of the two boys and appeared unexpectedly pleased with Bruno, who had taken the trouble to make sure that her child wasn't born with a craving for coconut. He's well brought up, she said, a student but not too boring: he seems not to care about how he's dressed but everything he has on, from his bathing suit to his shirt and sandals, is expensive. She appeared curious about the fact that someone could be wealthy in a fashion different from that of her brother, Rino, the Solaras. She made a remark that struck me: At the bar on the beach he bought me this and that without showing off.

Her mother-in-law, who, for the entire length of that vacation, never went to the beach but took care of the shopping, the house, preparing dinner and also the lunch that we carried to the beach the next day, listened as if her daughter-in-law were recounting to her an enchanted world. Naturally she noticed immediately that her daughter was preoccupied, and kept glancing at her questioningly. But Lila was distracted. She caused no trouble of any type, she allowed Pinuccia to sleep with her again, she wished everyone good night. Then she did something completely unexpected. I had just gone to bed when she appeared in the little room.

"Will you give me one of your books?" she asked.

I looked at her in bewilderment. She wanted to read? How long since she had opened a book, three, four years? And why now had she decided to start again? I took the volume of Beckett, the one I used to kill the mosquitoes, and gave it to her. It seemed the most accessible text I had.

CONTRIBUTORS' NOTES

SHANNON BURNS is the author of *Preserving the Old Way of Life*. She's a student in the MFA program at UMass-Amherst and Managing Editor of jubilat. She's from the Ozarks but now lives in Northampton, Massachusetts with her husband, Jacob.

SARA BATKIE was born in Seattle, has lived in Connecticut and Iowa, and currently resides in Brooklyn. She is a 2010 graduate of New York University's Masters in Fiction Writing program. Her stories have been published in Gulf Coast and LIT magazine and received mention in the 2011 edition of Best American Short Stories. She recently completed work on her first novel.

LYDIA CONKLIN is a recipient of a Pushcart Prize and fellowships from the MacDowell Colony, Bread Loaf, the James Merrill House, the Vermont Studio Center, Millay, Jentel, the Astraea Foundation, the Santa Fe Art Institute, Caldera, the Sitka Center and Harvard University, among others. Her fiction has appeared in Narrative Magazine, New Letters, The New Orleans Review, and elsewhere, and is forthcoming from The Southern Review and FiveChapters. She has drawn graphic fiction for Gulf Coast, Salt Hill and the Steppenwolf Theater in Chicago. She holds an MFA from the University of Wisconsin-Madison.

PAUL CRENSHAW's stories and essays have appeared or are forthcoming in *Best American Essays 2005* and *2011*, anthologies by W.W. Norton and Houghton Mifflin, Ecotone, Glimmer Train, North American Review, and Southern Humanities Review, among others. He teaches writing and literature at Elon University.

ANDREW DURBIN is the author of *Mature Themes* (Nightboat Books 2015) as well as several chapbooks, including *Believers* (Poor Claudia 2013) and *the islands* (Insert Blanc Press 2014). With Ben Fama, he edits Wonder, an open-source publishing and events platform for innovative writing, performance, and new media art. He lives in New York.

JESS DUTSCHMANN is the author of two books of poetry, *Calamity* and *Titanic*, and is a co-curator of the Artificial City NYC reading series. She is widely published online, and won "Best of the Net" by Sundress Publications in 2011. She lives in Jersey City, next to a little food place that in the morning smells like bacon and at night smells like beer.

CONTRIBUTORS' NOTES

ELENA FERRANTE was born in Naples. She is the author of *The Days of Abandonment*, which the New York Times called "stunning;" *My Brilliant Friend* which James Wood, in The New Yorker, described as "large, captivating, amiably peopled . . . a beautiful and delicate tale of confluence and reversal;" and two other novels, *Troubling Love* and *The Lost Daughter*. *The Story of a New Name* will be published by Europa Editions.

TAYLOR FOX was born in Colorado and grew up in Kalamazoo, Michigan. He attended the University of Michigan and every home football game during his four years in Ann Arbor. After receiving his law degree from Indiana University he moved to Phoenix, Arizona, where he currently resides and has a solo criminal defense practice. He remains a loyal—and occasionally manic—follower of Michigan football. "Not for Public Display" is his first published work.

CEAN GAMALINDA is an artist living in downtown Nebraska. He is the author of *Crowthoughts* (Penguin Books, 2007), *Crowthoughts* (University of Chicago Press, 2010), and *Crowthoughts* (University of Chicago Press, 2013).

ANN GOLDSTEIN's translations for Europa Editions include two novels by Amara Lakhous, two books by Alessandro Piperno, including *The Worst Intentions*, and five novels by Elena Ferrante. She is currently editing the complete works of Primo Levi for W.W. Norton. She is head of the copy department at The New Yorker and lives in New York.

LAURA GOLDSTEIN has published six chapbooks as well as poetry and essays in the Denver Quarterly, American Letters and Commentary, How2, Jacket2 and other fine publications. She teaches Writing and Literature at Loyola University and is the co-curator of the Red Rover Series with Jennifer Karmin. Her first collection of poetry, *loaded arc* has recently been released by Trembling Pillow Press.

DEBBIE HU's blog is http://areyouoverityet.tumblr.com and she tweets as @debbiehu. She has a book out from Perfect Lovers Press called *AIRY BABY: AN EQUAL TO THE ATE NIPPLE?//I worry/I don't/ Believe in Books/or do owly///*.

JASON KATZENSTEIN is a short, nebbishy 23-year-old graduate of Wesleyan University. When he was young he dreamed of playing for the NBA but had to give that dream up because see first sentence. Now he draws comics about angry old men and their starry-eyed grandchildren. You can find his work in MAD, Scene, and Scooter Magazine, and at jasonkatzenstein.webs.com.

189

SUE LANDERS is the author of *248 mgs., a panic picnic* (O Books, 2003), *Covers* (O Books, 2007), *15: A Poetic Engagement with the Chicago Manual of Style* (Least Weasel, 2011), and *What I Was Tweeting While You Were On Facebook* (Perfect Lovers, 2013). Her latest project, a mash up of *The Autobiography of Benjamin Franklin*, Gertrude Stein's *The Making of Americans* and the history of one Philadelphia neighborhood, is called *Franklinstein*. She blogs about her work at susanlanders.tumblr.com.

KELIN LOE is the author of the chapbook *The Motorist* (minutes BOOKS, 2010). Recent work can be found in jubilat and NOO Weekly. She is a cofounder of SPOKE TOO SOON: A Journal of the Longer and the host of Flying Object Radio. She lives in Northampton, MA with Michael.

NATASHA LVOVICH is a writer and scholar of bilingualism and of translingual literature— literature written in non-native language. Originally from Moscow, Russia, she teaches at City University of New York and divides her loyalties between academic and creative writing. She is an author of a collection of autobiographical narratives, *The Multilingual Self*, and of a number of articles and essays. Her creative nonfiction appeared in academic journals (Life Writing, New Writing), anthologies (Lifewriting Annual, Anthology of Imagination & Place) and literary magazines (Big.City.Lit, Post Road, Paradigm, Nashville Review, Two Bridges, bioStories, NDQ). Her essay, "Balakovo," was nominated for a Pushcart Prize.

LAURA MARIE MARCIANO is a poet, writer, performer and media artist concerned with beauty, oddity, pop culture, and social equity. She has been published in print and online and teaches at Fairfield University. Born and raised in Providence, Rhode Island she now resides in Brooklyn. She can be found at www.lauramariemarciano.tumblr.com.

FILIP MARINOVICH is the author of *And If I Don't Go Crazy I'll Meet You Here Tomorrow, Zero Readership*, and the forthcoming *Wolfman Librarian*, all from Ugly Duckling Presse. He teaches his READING POETS BY SUN SIGN poetry workshop at the Poetry Project at St Marks Church, Ugly Duckling Presse at the Old American Can Factory, and other hospitable locations. He was the co-compiler, with Stephen Boyer, of *The Occupy Wall Street Poetry Anthology*, and one of the librarians at The People's Library at Zuccotti Park. His work appears in EOAGH, The Brooklyn Rail, Aufgabe, Elective Affinities, Overpass Books, and Poetry Society of America. Visit him online at wolfmanlibrarian.blogspot.com.

MIRANDA MCLEOD's fiction has appeared in Willow Springs, The Sunday Times, Confrontation, The Bridport Anthology, Evolver, and elsewhere. She won the Bridport Flash Fiction Prize and was shortlisted for the Glimmer Train and Tanne Foundation fiction awards. She is a Fellow of the Kimbilio Center for African American Fiction, the Pirogue Collective and the Hurston/Wright Foundation. Miranda studied creative writing at Columbia University, earned an MFA in Fiction at New York University and is currently earning her Ph.D. in Literature at Rutgers University. She teaches creative writing at the Bryant Park Word for Word series.

BENJAMIN T. MILLER earned his MFA in Fiction from UC Irvine, and his work has appeared recently in ZYZZYVA and the Santa Monica Review. He lives in Los Angeles, where he teaches English at Pasadena City College and is writing a novel.

EDITH PEARLMAN was the recipient of the 2011 PEN/Malamud award for excellence in short fiction, honoring her four collections of stories: *Vaquita*, *Love Among the Greats*, *How To Fall*, and *Binocular Vision*. *Binocular Vision* received several other awards. It was published in the UK by Pushkin Press in 2013. Recent work has recently or will soon appear in, among other places, The Antioch Review, The American Scholar, The Harvard Review, Ecotone, and Orion; and in the anthology, A Story Larger than My Own.

STEVE ROGGGENBOOK is the first poet to be catalogued as a meme by the popular website Know Your Meme. His most recent book is called "IF U DONT LOVE THE MOON YOUR AN ASS HOLE." His website is livemylief.com. :)

MATTHEW SOCIA has received a scholarship to the Bread Loaf Writers' Conference, and a 2013 Emerging Writer Fellowship to the Writers' Room of Boston. He is an MFA candidate in fiction at Emerson College. His writing also appears in CutBank.

SAMUEL TOLZMANN's visual artwork — including drawings, artist's books, prints, animated films, watercolor, embroidery, and sculpture — has been featured in a number of solo and group exhibitions as well as printed journals, most of them collegiate. He was born in Burlington, Vermont and educated in literature at Middlebury College and the University of Oxford (Lincoln College). Currently a contributing critic for the popular music website Pretty Much Amazing, he resides in Northampton, Massachusetts.

RUVANEE PIETERSZ VILHAUER was born in Sri Lanka, and now lives in the U.S. She won the Commonwealth Short Story Prize in 2004. Her stories have appeared or are forthcoming in The Kenyon Review, Stand, Notre Dame Review, Quiddity, The Summerset Review, The Fourth River, and elsewhere. She teaches in the Psychology department at Felician College in New Jersey. Her website is www.ruvaneevilhauer.com.

KIM VODICKA is the author of *Aesthesia Balderdash* (Trembling Pillow 2012). She holds an M.F.A. in creative writing from Louisiana State University (2013). Her artwork has been published in Tenderloin, and her poems have been published in Shampoo, Ekleksographia, Dig, Spork, Unlikely Stories, RealPoetik, and TheThe Poetry.

DOUGLAS WATSON is the author of a book of stories, *The Era of Not Quite*. His novel, *A Moody Fellow Finds Love and Then Dies*, will be published in 2014 by Outpost19. He lives in New York City.

SIMONE WHITE is the author of *Unrest* (Ugly Duckling Presse, Dossier Series), *House Envy of All of the World* (Factory School) and *Dolly* (Q Ave Press, with the paintings of Kim Thomas). Recent work appears in The Baffler, The Brooklyn Rail, and Big Bell. She lives in Bedford-Stuyvesant, Brooklyn.

CASEY WILEY's essays and stories have been published or are forthcoming in Barrellhouse, Salt Hill, Gulf Stream, The Chronicle of Higher Education, Pindledyboz, Monkeybicycle, among others. He teaches English at Penn State University and is working on a novel about a failing American carnival.